Black Butler

XII

YANA TOBOSO

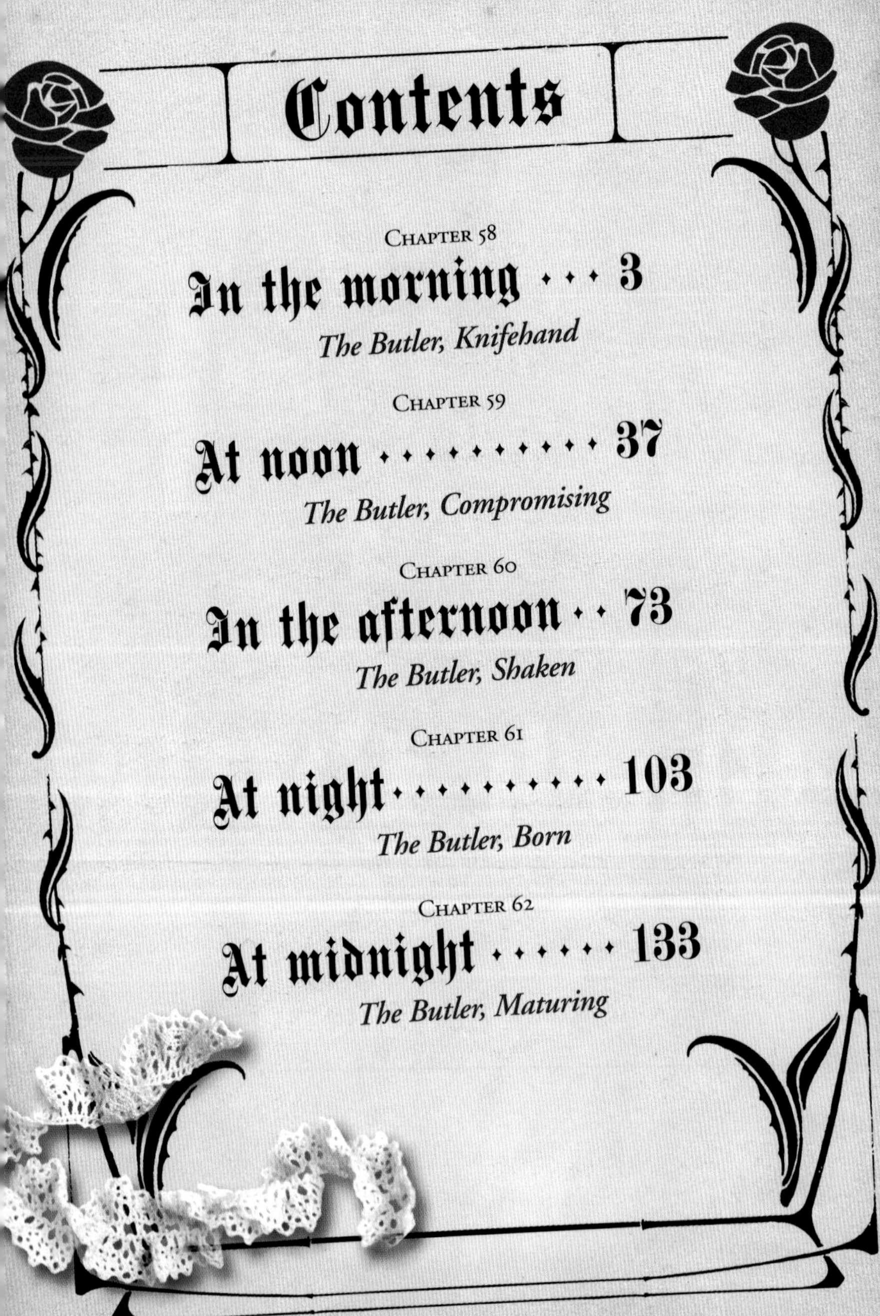

Contents

Chapter 58
In the morning : The Butler, Knifehand

What are
little girls made of?
"Sugar and spice,
and all that's nice;
And that's what little
girls are made of."

A LADY...

...SHOULD ALWAYS BE DELICATE AND LOVELY BEFORE A GENTLEMAN...

...AN INNOCENT GIRL FIRST AND FOREMOST.

HER JOB IS TO BE SURROUNDED BY ALL THINGS NICE LIKE MOTHER GOOSE'S NURSERY RHYME SAYS AND KEEP SMILING.

SO...

...STAY LIKE THAT FOR AS LONG AS YOU POSSIBLY CAN.

I WILL!

Poetry over philosophy.
Embroidery over cooking.
Dancing over chess.

Be an angel who knows nothing.

That is how girls born into a nation of roses are raised.

I WAS JUST LIKE THAT TOO.
ELIZA-BETH.
IT IS TIME.
BUT—

I STOOD APART FROM OTHER GIRLS IN ONE RESPECT.

ざわ
ZAWA (MURMUR)
KAKIN (CLANG)
ざわ
ZAWA
KIIN (CLANG)

SO THAT IS THE SON OF THE MARQUESS OF MIDFORD, WHO IS RUMOURED TO BE A GENIUS WITH SWORDS.
KIIN
HUNH?
WHAT ARE YOU SAYING, PHIPPS?
TOUCHÉ!!

ZAWA

THE GENIUS IS THE DAUGHTER.

WAA
(CHEER)

WHAT I DANCED AT VARIOUS HALLS WAS NOT THE WALTZ.

WAAH!!
DOTA
(THUD)

YOUR ADVANCE IS WEAK, CIEL!!
BUT, VERY WELL.
THAT'S ENOUGH FOR TODAY.

UGGGH... SHE WAS SCARY...

MOTHER'S VERY STRICT!

AUNT FRANCIS IS A BEAUTIFUL LADY, BUT...

...IF MY WIFE WAS THAT STRONG...

...I THINK I WOULD BE FRIGHT-ENED OF HER.

ドキッ

DOKI (BADUMP)

I'M SO GLAD IT'S YOU WHO'LL BE MY BRIDE, LIZZIE!

MY DEAR, ADORABLE FIANCÉ, YOUNGER THAN ME BY A YEAR.
THAT'S WHEN I MADE A VOW.

I would become a bride Ciel could protect.
NO!!
NO! I SAID, NO!
PAN (SLAP)
YOU ARE A GIRL WHO IS TO MARRY INTO THE HOUSE OF PHANTOMHIVE.
YOU WILL NOT BE ALLOWED TO NEGLECT YOUR TRAINING!

I WON'T PRACTISE FENCING ANYMORE!

SWORDS AREN'T CUTE AT ALL!!

ギュッ

GYU (HUG)

EVEN IF YOU DO FIND IT TRYING, IT'S FOR YOUR SAKE, AND HIS...

YOU UNDERSTAND, DON'T YOU?

BUT THAT DAY...

ADVENT
CALENDER

AWW, CIEL.
I WONDER IF HE'LL LIKE HIS BIRTHDAY PRESENT!

LADY LIZZIE!

THE PHANTOMHIVE FAMILY HAS BEEN...

BAN (WHAM)

IT WAS MY DREAM TO BECOME A LOVELY WIFE WHO WOULD BE PROTECTED BY CIEL.

BUT THAT DREAM WAS NEVER TO COME TRUE.

LADIES, HAVE YOU HEARD?

THE HORRIFIC SLAUGHTER OF THE PHANTOMHIVE FAMILY!

IN ALL LIKELIHOOD, THEY MUST HAVE RAISED SOMEONE'S IRE, NO?

GRACIOUS, HOW FRIGHTFUL!

BY THE WAY, IT SEEMS LADY ASHLEY HAS HERSELF YET ANOTHER NEW LOVER.

MY... SHE IS QUITE ENERGETIC.

IN JET-BLACK WEEDS...

...AND IN THE JET-BLACKEST OF MOODS...

...A BLEAK, JET-BLACK WINTER MONTH PASSED. AND THEN...

...WITH A BUTLER CLOTHED BLACK AS JET.

I CAN'T BELIEVE MY EYES!!

IT REALLY IS YOU, ISN'T IT, CIEL!?

......

SO (SLIDE)

I'M BACK...

...ELIZA-BETH.

THE CIEL WHO CAME BACK TO ME WAS THINNER AND SMALLER THAN I.
BUT I SOON REALISED SOME-THING.
CIEL HADN'T BECOME SMALLER. IT WAS I WHO HAD GROWN BIGGER.
AND SO I MADE A NEW VOW.
I would become a bride who could protect Ciel.

BUT... I REALLY WOULD RATHER BE CUTE.

LOOK, PAULA!
AREN'T THESE JUST THE CUTEST!?

FATHER BOUGHT THEM FOR ME AS A REWARD FOR WINNING MY FENCING BOUT!
I THINK I'LL WEAR THEM TODAY SINCE I'M GOING OUT WITH CIEL!
MY, MY! HOW VERY WONDERFUL!

OH!

LADY LIZZIE, HAVE YOU GOTTEN A BIT TALLER AGAIN?

EH...?

AH...!
I—! I DO BEG YOUR PARDON!

AH! UM!
ORO (PANIC)
ORO
YOU ARE STILL LOVELY AND ADORABLE EVEN IF YOU HAVE GROWN, MY LADY!
......

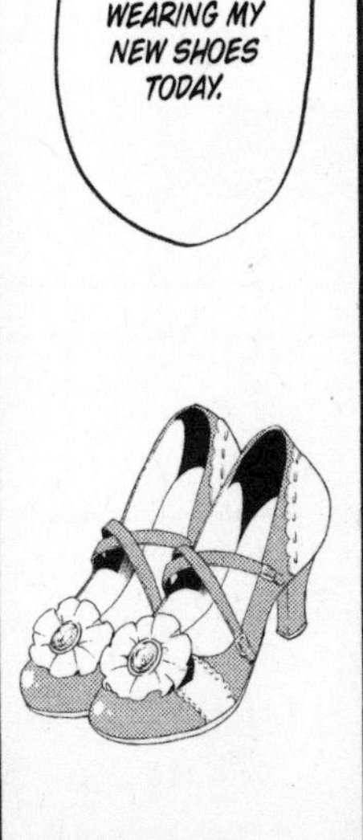
I WON'T BE WEARING MY NEW SHOES TODAY.

BUT...
LEAVE IT. JUST GET ME A PAIR WITH LOW HEELS, PAULA.

GIRLS MY AGE ALL WEAR CUTE HIGH HEELS, BUT...

...FOR THE SAKE OF CIEL, WHO IS PUSHING HIMSELF TO GROW UP FAST...
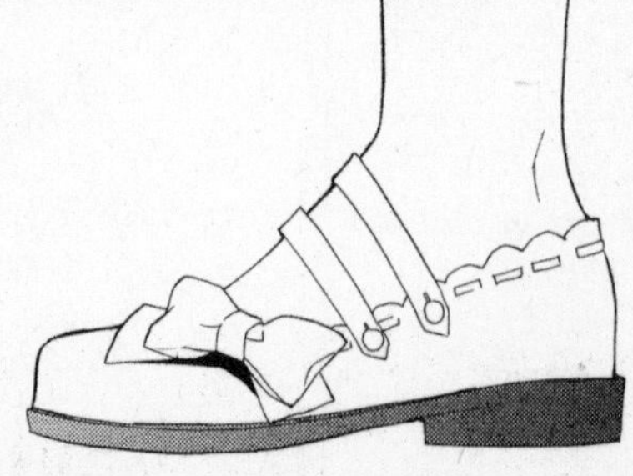
...I WEAR MY CHILDISH, LOW-HEELED SHOES AND SMILE BESIDE HIM.

ZAZAA
(SKSKSH)
LOW-HEELED SHOES.
MOTHER'S LESSONS.
SWORDS WITH WHICH TO PROTECT YOU.

THAT...

...IS WHAT I AM MADE OF.

KI
(GLARE)
I'M FINE WITH NOT BEING CUTE...
BA
(LUNGE)
...IF IT MEANS I CAN PROTECT YOU!!

MY LADY.
YOU HAVE DONE ENOUGH...

SEBAS...
...TIAN?
HAAH ...!

TO HAVE FORCED A LADY TO GO TO SUCH LENGTHS AS THESE...

I AM A FAILURE AS A BUTLER.

PLEASE FORGIVE ME.

I SHALL HANDLE THE REST...
SU (SLIP)
ZAAAA (SHAAA)

MMMM, I DO FEEL A BIT LIKE THE WIND WAS TAKEN OUT OF MY SAILS, BUT...
ZAAAA
...NO MATTER!
LET'S PICK UP WHERE WE LEFT OFF, HMM...?
HA (GASP)

BITA (FREEZE)

WAIT! SEBASTIAN!!

WE CAN'T AFFORD TO DEAL WITH THEM RIGHT NOW!

RIAN IS THE ONE WHO HOLDS ALL THE KEYS TO THIS CASE!

WE'RE GOING AFTER HIM!

HUNH?

HEY, YOU.
RIAN, RIAN...
ARE YOU SAYING WE CAN GET TO THE BOTTOM OF THE REANIMATED CORPSES IF WE PUT THE SCREWS ON THIS RIAN CHAP?

MISTER SUTCLIFF, LOOK.
NNNN?

I SEE.

IT SEEMS WE CAN'T AFFORD TO PLAY WITH YOU EITHER.

TO (LEAP)

IT DOES SOOOO PAIN ME, BUT I FEAR WE'LL HAVE TO PART HERE FOR NOW, SEBASTIAN DARLING.

SUTO (LAND)

HIRARI (FLAP)

NCHU (SMOOCH)
NEXT TIME I'LL BE SURE TO WRAP YOU ALL UP IN ROSY RED! COUNT! ON! IT! ♡
TOODLES! ♡

WE SHOULD HURRY TOO—
UGH!
ZUKI (THROB)
YOUNG MASTER!

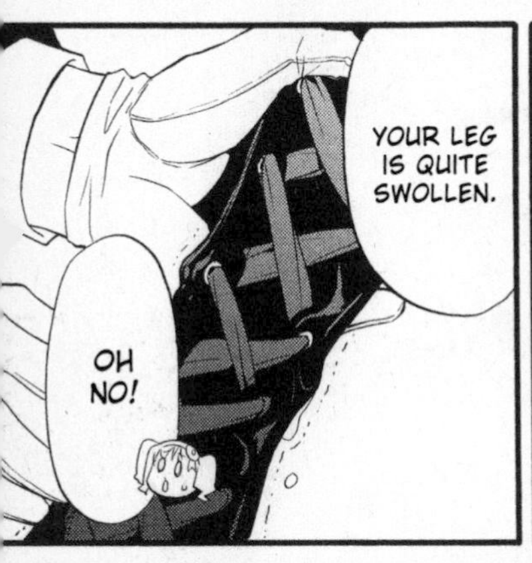
YOUR LEG IS QUITE SWOLLEN.
OH NO!

I'LL CARRY YOU ON MY BACK!
WHA—!?
GAN (SHOCK)

LADY ELIZABETH, I CAN TAKE CARE OF THAT...
I TRULY CANNOT ALLOW YOU TO DO SUCH A THING...
AH!
OH, YES! OF COURSE. YOU'RE RIGHT! OH, DEAR, WHAT HAS COME OVER ME!?
I...

BUWA (TEARY)

GYO (SHOCK)

!?

UWAAAAAH!
I'M THE SORT OF SCARY GIRL CIEL DESPISES ~~~!
HUNH !?

UWAAAAAAH!
WHAT ARE YOU TALKING ABOUT!?
WELL, YOU SAID BEFORE THAT YOU DIDN'T WANT A STRONG, SCARY WIIIIFE!

TH-THAT WAS A LONG TIME AGO.
BESIDES, I'M THE ONE WHO SHOULD BE APOLO-GISING TO YOU.
THEN WILL YOU STILL MARRY ME?
YOU HAVEN'T COME TO HATE ME?

HOW COULD I POS-SIBLY HATE Y...
HA (GASP)

KAAAA (BLUSH)

N—
NOW ISN'T THE TIME FOR THIS!
WE'RE HEADING UPSTAIRS, C'MON!!
BUHA (SPUTTER)

EVEN THE YOUNG MASTER CANNOT HOLD HIS OWN AGAINST HIS LADY, I SEE.

KUH! KUH! KUH ...!

SHUT YOUR MOUTH, YOU!!

?

OHHHH, H-HOW VERY AMUSING...

WELL, THEN. LET US BE OFF.

YOU BASTARD. ARE YOU QUITE DONE GIGGLING YE—

SMILE!

SNAKE.

I TRULY AM SO GLAD EVERYONE IS SAFE.
—SAYS EMILY.
WHERE'S RIAN?
SORRY, HE RAN AWAY ON US.
—SAYS OSCAR.
IS THAT SO ...?
BASHA (SPLASH)

WELL, LET US REGROUP WITH THE MARQUESS AND HIS FAMILY FOR THE MOMENT.
ZAAAA (SHAAAA)
YEAH.

THE CAMPANIA
First-Class Deck

ZAWA (CLAMOUR)

ZAWA

BACK OFF!!

WOMEN AND CHILDREN FIRST!

JUST LOOK AT THE SIGHT OF YOU! HOW CAN YOU CALL YOURSELVES BRITISH GENTLEMEN!?

EDWARD!!

LIZZIE!!

GASHI (GRAB)

I'M SO HAPPY TO SEE YOU WELL!!

...IT MUST HAVE BEEN HARD FOR YOU...

ZAWA
FORGIVE ME. IT WAS ENTIRELY DUE TO MY HELP-LESSNESS.
ZAWA
YOU SAID IT!

BUT FINE, MY LECTURE CAN WAIT.
NOW YOU TWO GET ON A BOAT, QUICK AS YOU CAN...
EDWARD, I HAVE A FAVOUR TO ASK OF YOU.

PUT HIM ON THE BOAT IN MY STEAD.

!?

I CAN'T GET ONTO A BOAT YET.

......

ALL RIGHT. WE'LL TAKE CARE OF HIM.

IF CIEL IS TO STAY BEHIND, I SHALL STAY T—!
TO (CHOP)
!?

I BEG YOUR PARDON, SIR.

BUTLER!!

IT APPEARED THAT CONVINCING LADY ELIZABETH WOULD TAKE SOME TIME, SO I RESORTED TO A ROUGH MEASURE.

PLEASE METE OUT WHATEVER PUNISHMENT YOU SEE FIT AT A LATER TIME.

NO... YOU HAVE MY THANKS. IT'S IMPOSSIBLE FOR ME TO ATTACK MY SISTER FROM BEHIND.

THE SHIP IS LISTING CONSIDERABLY...

ITS FOUNDERING IS BUT A MATTER OF TIME.

PLEASE LEAVE THE SHIP WITH THE UTMOST URGENCY AND GET AS FAR AWAY FROM IT AS YOU POSSIBLY CAN.

TAKE CARE OF LIZZIE AND SNAKE!

ZAWA (CLAMOUR)
ZAWA
LET'S GO, SEBAS-TIAN.
VERY GOOD, SIR.

YOU DON'T NEED TO COME BACK, YOU KNOW!!

I'M PERFECTLY FINE WITH NOT HAVING TO GIVE AWAY MY ADORABLE LITTLE SISTER'S HAND!

I SHALL RETURN, I ASSURE YOU.

THE CAMPANIA
First-Class Hall
GII (CREAK)
DAMN! THE SHIP'S LISTING LIKE CRAZY.
WHERE IS HE ...!?
GII
ZARARA (SLIDE)
GASHAN (CRASH)
GURA (SWAY)
UWAH ...!
!?

がしっ
GASHI (GRAB)
OOOH, I SAY! YOU'RE QUITE A CATCH, DEAR BOY!
!?
I'VE GOT YOU HOOK, LINE, AND SINKER! ♡

Black Butler

Chapter 59
At noon : The Butler, Compromising

PAAAN (BLAM)
PAAAAN

SET OFF ALL THE FIREWORKS AND DISTRESS FLARES WE HAVE ABOARD!
KEEP THE SHIP LIT!
WE'VE RECEIVED A TRANS-MISSION FROM A CARGO VESSEL SAILING NEARBY.

THEY CAN REACH US IN ABOUT TWO HOURS IF THEY HURRY.
...IS THAT SO!
ALL WE CAN DO NOW IS GET AS MANY PEOPLE ON THE BOATS AS HUMANLY POSSIBLE.
WAAA (SHRIEK)
DO IT QUICK!
AYE-AYE, SIR!
WAAAA
GOBOBO (GLUBUB)
ZUZUZU (FWOOSH)

PAAAN
PAAAN
PAAAN
TWO MORE HOURS, EH...?

THE CAMPANIA
First-Class Lounge

SO YOU'RE RIAN, HM?

WHA—!? HOW DO YOU KNOW MY NAM—

OKAY, OKAY! THAT'S ENOUGH SMALL TALK.

ARE WE RIGHT IN ASSUMING YOU'RE THE FELLOW WHO DOCTORED THE CORPSES TO MAKE THEM MOVE?

!

チラッ
CHIRA (PEEK)
SUCH A PAIN, AREN'T THEY? THESE "IRREGULAR" TYPES.

"DEATH" IS S'POSED TO BE A RULE THAT CAN NEVER BE OVERTURNED IN THIS WORLD.

WELL?
HOW DO YOU STOP THOSE CORPSES?

TH—
THERE'S A DEVICE IN MY ROOM THAT WILL NULLIFY THEIR ABSOLUTE SALVATION!!

—SO?

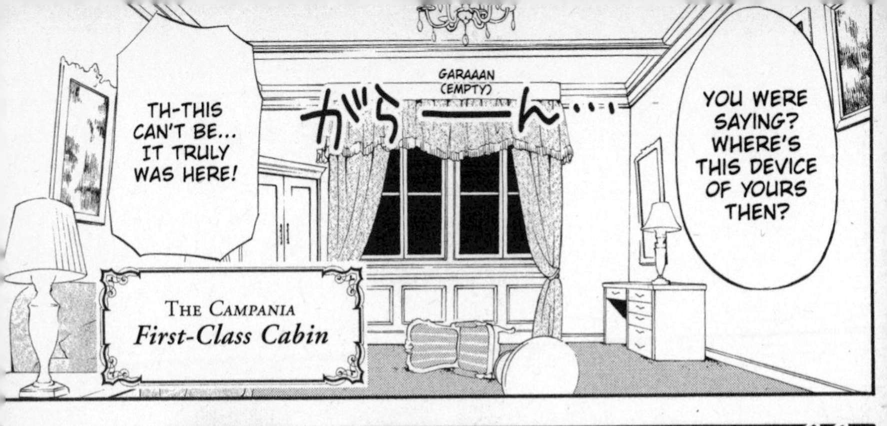
YOU WERE SAYING? WHERE'S THIS DEVICE OF YOURS THEN?
GARAAAN (EMPTY)
がらーーん…
TH-THIS CAN'T BE... IT TRULY WAS HERE!
THE CAMPANIA
First-Class Cabin

HA (GASP)

DON'T TELL ME ...!!

C DECK
THE CAMPANIA
Corridor, First-Class Cabins

THAT MAN MADE OFF WITH IT...!?
ZA (STEP)
C DECK

YOU'RE —!!

THE VISCOUNT OF DRUITT...!?

NN? AND WHO ARE YOU?
HOW DO YOU KNOW WHO I AM?

ギクッ
GIKU (GULP)

WELL, I SUPPOSE IT IS INDEED DIFFICULT TO NOT KNOW OF ME, AS I'M CELEBRATED IN SOCIETY CIRCLES FOR BEING THE PERSONIFICATION OF BEAUTY.
SARA (SWISH)
サラッ

WITH ALL DUE RESPECT, WHAT ARE YOU DOING IN A PLACE LIKE THIS, VISCOUNT?
THE WALKING DEAD ARE AMBLING THROUGH THIS VESSEL AS WE SPEAK.

ふっ
HEH!

THERE'S SOMETHING HERE THAT I DAREN'T LEAVE ON THIS SINKING SHIP, EVEN IF IT MEANS EXPOSING MYSELF TO MORTAL DANGER.

TO BEGIN WITH, THOSE CORPSES AMOUNT TO NOTHING MORE THAN USELESS DOLLS TO ME—
OH, DEAR.
I'VE NATTERED ON FOR TOO LONG... IF YOU'LL EXCUSE ME.

THE ETERNAL FLAME IN THIS BREAST!
HA (GASP)
CAN-NOT BE QUENCHED BY ANY-ONE!
WE ARE—
PHOENIX!!!

AH! SO YOU WERE COMRADES! SPEAKING OF, I DO GET THE FEELING WE'VE MET BEFORE.

!!

THAT CONTRAP-TION!

CAN IT PERHAPS STOP THE MOVEMENTS OF THOSE CORPSES?

WHERE DID YOU LEARN THAT?

I KNEW IT...
THEN YOU'RE—!?

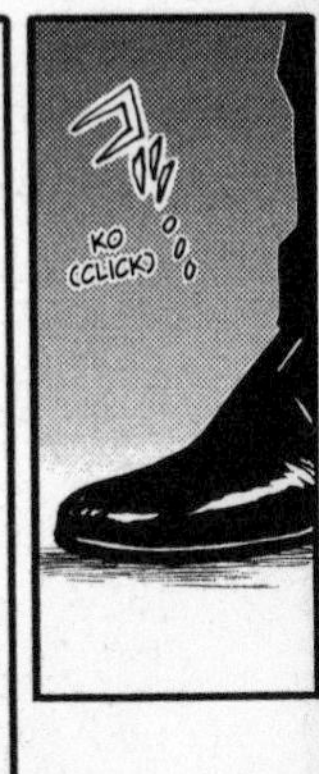
KO (CLICK)

IF YOU WISH TO KNOW, FOLLOW ME.
I SHALL ALLOW YOU TO BEAR WITNESS AS WELL.

TO THE ADVENT OF A NEW AURORA BY WAY OF MEDICINE...
...THAT IS.

KO
KO (CLICK)

SHALL WE TAKE IT BY FORCE, SIR?
NO, WE DON'T KNOW HOW TO USE IT.
LET'S HAVE HIM ACTIVATE IT FOR U—

GUH HEE HEE...

WHAT THE—!? UNDER-TAKER!?
WHAT ARE YOU DOING HERE?
HEE! HEE!
HIIIYA!

I WAS TOLD TO HELP CARRY THIS AS I WAS IN THE MIDDLE OF RUNNING FOR MY LIFE, YOU SEEEE!
THEN I CAUGHT SIGHT OF THE EARL HOLLERING "PHOENIX" ONCE MORE, AND...
WIPE THAT FROM YOUR MEMORY RIGHT NOW!!

HISO (PSSST)
But more importantly, do you have a clue as to how to work this thing?

CAN'T SAY THAT I DOOO?
I WONDER IF SOMETHING LIKE THIS SERVES ANY USEFUL PURPOSE AT ALL, YOU KNOW?

THE CAMPANIA
First-Class Lounge

BE VERY CAUTIOUS WITH IT. IT IS WORTH MORE THAN YOUR LIVES.

WILL YOU START IT UP NOW?
NOT YET.

OUR CAST IS STILL ONE PLAYER SHORT.

?
ONE PLAYER?
AH!

YOU RAT!!

WHY DID YOU STEAL THE DEVICE !!?

HELLO THERE, RIAN.
I'VE BEEN WAITING FOR YOU!
THIS DAY SHALL MARK THE FALL OF YOUR EMPIRE IN ONE NIGHT, AS POMPEII ONCE FELL...
...AND THE DAY MY NEW EMPIRE WAS BORN!
EH!?
WITH THE POWER OF THIS DEVICE...
...I SHALL BUILD A NEW EMPIRE!!

COME AGAIN?
HE WHO POSSESSES ETERNITY SHALL RULE WITH IMMORALITY AND DECADENT BEAUTY.
AND IT SHALL BE CALLED—
THE AURORA EMPIRE!!
BA (BAM)
THIS ALL SEEMS TO HAVE GONE KINDA PEAR-SHAPED, HUH?
WHAT THE HECK?
HMPH.
I'LL MAKE THAT CAD THE REDDEST OF REDS IN THE BLINK OF AN EYE!
EASY NOW!!

DON'T YOU CARE WHAT HAPPENS TO THIS MACHINE?

SU (SWF)

!!

HEY, MISTER SUTCLIFF, TIME OUT!!

GABA (GRAB)

FU-FU... THIS IS WHAT IS CALLED TRUE "POWER."

I CAN STAND VICTORIOUS AGAINST YOU ALL WITH NOTHING MORE THAN A SINGLE WINE-GLASS!!

FWAH-HA-HA-HA-HA!

THIS SENSE OF IRRITATION JUST GROWS AND GROWS. MAY I KILL HIM, YOUNG MASTER?
NO, NOT YET. THOUGH I DO UNDER-STAND HOW YOU FEEL...

GASHAN (CRASH)
OOOOO (MOOOAN)
WHA—!?

おぉぉおぉお
HEY...! JUST LOOK AT THESE NUMBERS!!

VIS-COUNT, START THE DEVICE! HURRY!!
NON!
I AM NO LONGER A VISCOUNT!

"KAISER"... I SHALL START THE DEVICE IF YOU CALL ME THAT...
...WITH THAT LOVELY LITTLE MOUTH OF YOURS, SO VERY LIKE A COCK ROBIN'S.

はあ?
HUNH?

LET'S KILL HIM NOW, AFTER ALL.
PLEASE WAIT. THOUGH I DO UNDERSTAND HOW YOU FEEL...

OOH... OOH!
GLADIATORS, WHO PUT THEIR FLESH AND BLOOD ON THE LINE, WHOSE LIVES SCATTER LIKE SO MANY FALLEN PETALS.
THIS PLACE IS JUST LIKE A CORRUPT COLISEUM.
GAZING OUT AS I SIP MY WINE, I TRULY AM...
...JUST LIKE EMPEROR NERO!

SFX: IRA (IRRITATED) IRA IRA IRA IRA

AAAAAARG,
CAN WE KILL HIM NOW!?
イライライライライラ
GYARARARARA (VREEEE)
DO YOU WANT TO GET SUSPENDED!?
LET ME GET THIS STRAIGHT... YOU JUST STOPPED ME, DIDN'T YOU!?

HEY, YOU! GET A MOVE ON, AND START THAT THING UP, WOULD YOU!?

HEH...!

VERY WELL.

THE TIME FOR THE FOUNDING OF MY EMPIRE IS UPON US AT LAST.

NOW, THEN. ALL OF YOU!

SHOW ME THE DANCE OF THE PHOENIX IN PLEDGING YOUR ALLEGIANCE TO YOUR KAISER!

RIGHT. KILL HIM.
DEAR, DEAR.
WILL YOU BE SATISFIED WITH NEVER LEARNING WHAT THAT GADGET IS FOR?
GUH! HEE HEE...

KUH ...!
GUH FU FU!
ぐふふ

WHAT IS IT?
COME, NOW!!

TH—
THE ETERNAL FLAME IN THIS BREAST...

...CANNOT BE QUENCHED BY ANYONE...

WE ARE!
THE NEW!

PHOENIX!!!

WELL PLAYED, COMRADES!

NOW I SHALL SHOW YOU...

...THE ARMY OF DEATH THAT BOWS BEFORE ME!!

カチッ

KACHI (CLICK)

し…ん

SHI...N (SILENCE)

EH?
HUH?
HN?

GUOOOOO (ROOOAR)
NOOOOON!!!

GYAAAH! HA! HA! HA! HA! HA! HA-HA-HA!
WHAT ARE YOU PLAYING AT!?

WHY, RIAN! THE DEVICE YOU CRAFTED IS USELESS!
GYAH-HA HA HA HA HA HA HA! HA
I-IT CAN'T BE!

WEREN'T YOU THE ONE WHO MADE THIS THING!?
KIRI (BLUNT)
THERE'S OBVIOUSLY NO WAY I COULD BUILD A CONTRAPTION LIKE THIS!
I SIMPLY BORROWED IT AT MY DISCRETION.
HEEEEE! HAAAAA!

YOU BASTARD! DID YOU DECEIVE ME!?

!?

HAH!
WHAT A FARCE THIS IS!
BA (LEAP)
ZA (SKRSH)

ZAN (SLICE)
WHOO-EE!
YEAH, HE REALLY IS SOMETHIN' ELS—
HEY, WAIT, MISTER SUT-CLIFF, SIR!!
WE REAPERS SHOULDN'T BE GOIN' AROUND KILLING HUMANS, REMEMBER ...!!?
GAKIIIN (CLANG)

WHA—!?
GYARARARA (VREEE)
HEE! HEE...! IT'S BEEN AGES SINCE I LAUGHED THIS HARD...
IN MY HUMBLE OPINION, LOSING SUCH AN AMUSING CHAP WOULD AMOUNT TO A *LOSS* FOR THIS WORLD.
RARA
WOULDN'T YOU AGREE WITH ME, HMM?
MY LITTLE GRIM REAPERS?

GYARARARA (VREEEE)
THE BLADE OF MY DEATH SCYTHE WON'T CUT THROUGH ...!?
GIIN (SHNNG)
BUWA (BLAST)
南無大師遍照金剛

!!
ZUA
(WHIZ)

PAAN
(SHATTER)

GUUH ...!
YOUNG MASTER!!
AAH.
HOW SAD IT IIIS...

...THAT LAUGHTER SHOULD VANISH FROM THIS PLACE.

Black Butler

AAH. HOW SAD IT IIIS...
...THAT LAUGHTER SHOULD VANISH FROM THIS PLACE.

Chapter 60
In the afternoon : The Butler, Shaken

Black Butler

UNDER-TAKER ...!?
GASHAAAN (CRAAASH)

HE MASKED HIS PRESENCE MOST SKILL-FULLY.
HIS "EYES" HAVE ALWAYS BEEN HIDDEN AS WELL, SO IT ESCAPED EVEN MY NOTICE.

ストッ
SUTO (HOP)
SAME HERE. HE FOOLED ME GOOD.
MISTER SUT-CLIFF, SIR! THOSE EYES...

YES.
THAT CHAR-TREUSE PHOSPHO-RESCENCE, WITHOUT A DOUBT, CAN ONLY BELONG TO...

...A GRIM REAPER!
HEE! HEE!
HOW NOSTALGIIIC! IT'S BEEN AT LEAST HALF A CENTURY SINCE I WAS LAST CALLED THAT.

THE UNDER-TAKER...
...IS A GRIM REAPER—!?
EXPLAIN YOURSELF, UNDER-TAKER!!
YOU SAID I COULD CONTROL THOSE CORPSES WITH THIS DEVICE!

!!
DID IIII NOW, TRULY?
SO YOU TRICKED ME...
WAS IT ALL A LIE!?
EVEN THE PART ABOUT SAILING TO AMERICA TO POPULARISE ABSOLUTE SALVATION... EVERY-THING!!?

WELL, YOU SEEEE... I FOUND IT COMICAL THAT YOU WERE EARNESTLY ATTEMPTING TO RESURRECT THE DEAD VIA MEDICAL SCIENCE...
YOU WERE JUST THE MAN OF TALENT FOR MY PURPOSES.

AND WHAT OF OUR SINGULAR DESIRE TO BRING THE WHOLE WORLD INTO HEALTH AND WELL-BEING THROUGH MEDICINE ...!?
THAT WAS YOUR DESIRE, RIIIGHT?

BESIDES!

YOU ARE NOT CAPABLE OF BRINGING THE DEAD BACK TO LIFE BY THE POWER OF THE MEDICAL KNOWLEDGE IN YOUR GRASP.

AND IT ALL CEASED TO BE MEDICINE IN THE FIRST PLACE THE MOMENT YOU BEGAN TO DEPEND ON MY TECH-NIQUES.

ONE WHO CONDUCTS PROCEDURES UPON HIS PATIENTS THAT HE HIMSELF DOES NOT UNDERSTAND CAN NO LONGER CALL HIMSELF A PHYSICIAN.

GAKU (COLLAPSE)
H-HOW COULD THIS BE...?

PON (PAT)
YOU WERE A GOOD LAD, NAIVELY BUYING ALL I SAID WITHOUT QUESTION.

SO YOU'RE SAYING THAT YOU MASTER-MINDED THE AURORA SOCIETY'S EXPERI-MENTS TO RESURRECT THE DEAD?

UNDER-TAKER!

THAT'S A SECRET. ♡

—IS WHAT I'D LIKE TO SAY, BUT YOU HAVE PAID FOR INFORMATION INNUMERABLE TIMES OVER WITH THAT PHOENIX POSE OF YOURS, EARL.
SO TELL YOU, I SHALL!
HEE! HEE ...

OOOOO (MOOOAN)

'TWAS INDEED I WHO PRODUCED THESE REANIMATED CORPSES.

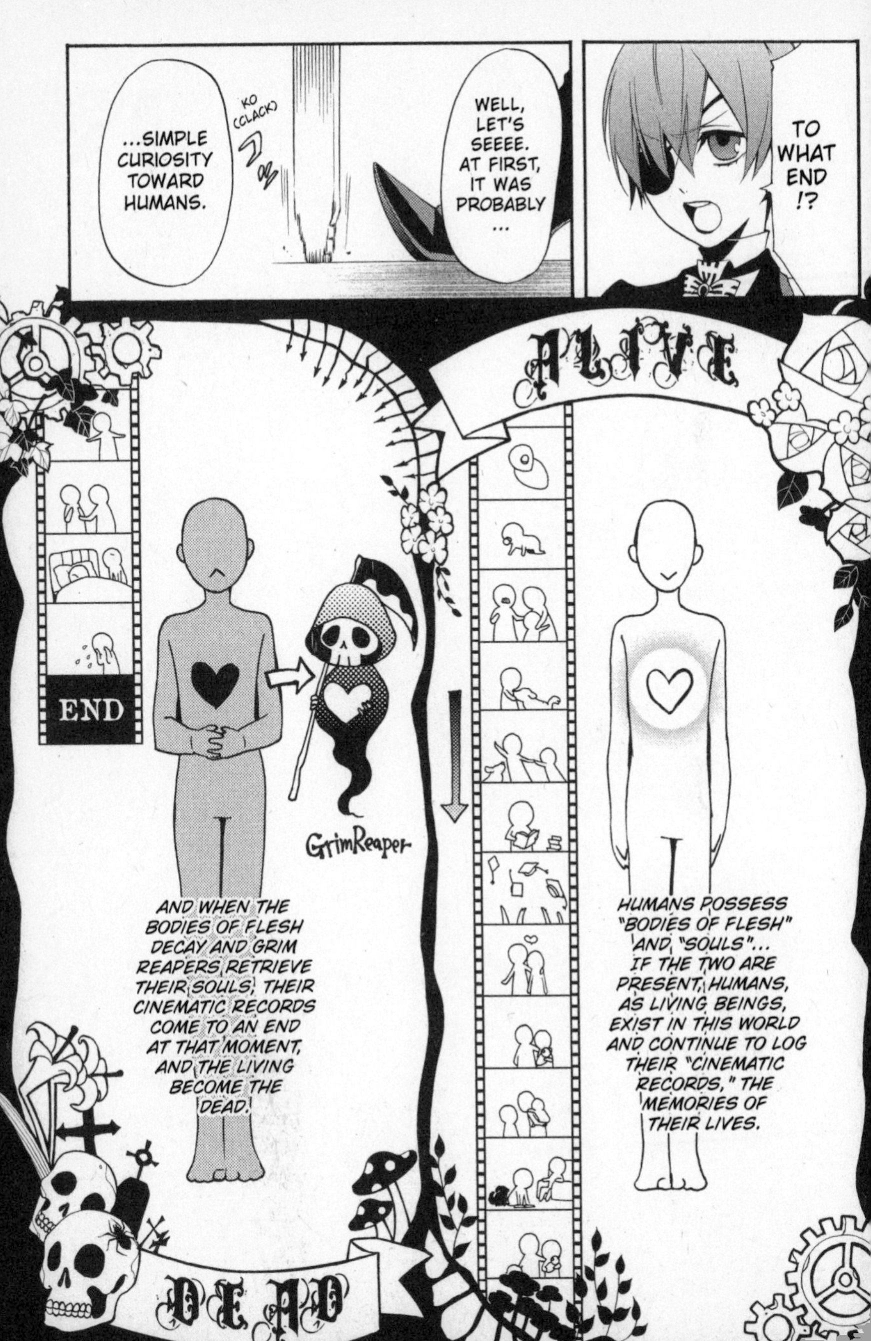
TO WHAT END!?
WELL, LET'S SEEEE. AT FIRST, IT WAS PROBABLY...
KO (CLACK)
...SIMPLE CURIOSITY TOWARD HUMANS.
ALIVE
HUMANS POSSESS "BODIES OF FLESH" AND "SOULS"... IF THE TWO ARE PRESENT, HUMANS, AS LIVING BEINGS, EXIST IN THIS WORLD AND CONTINUE TO LOG THEIR "CINEMATIC RECORDS," THE MEMORIES OF THEIR LIVES.
END
GrimReaper
AND WHEN THE BODIES OF FLESH DECAY AND GRIM REAPERS RETRIEVE THEIR SOULS, THEIR CINEMATIC RECORDS COME TO AN END AT THAT MOMENT, AND THE LIVING BECOME THE DEAD.
DEAD

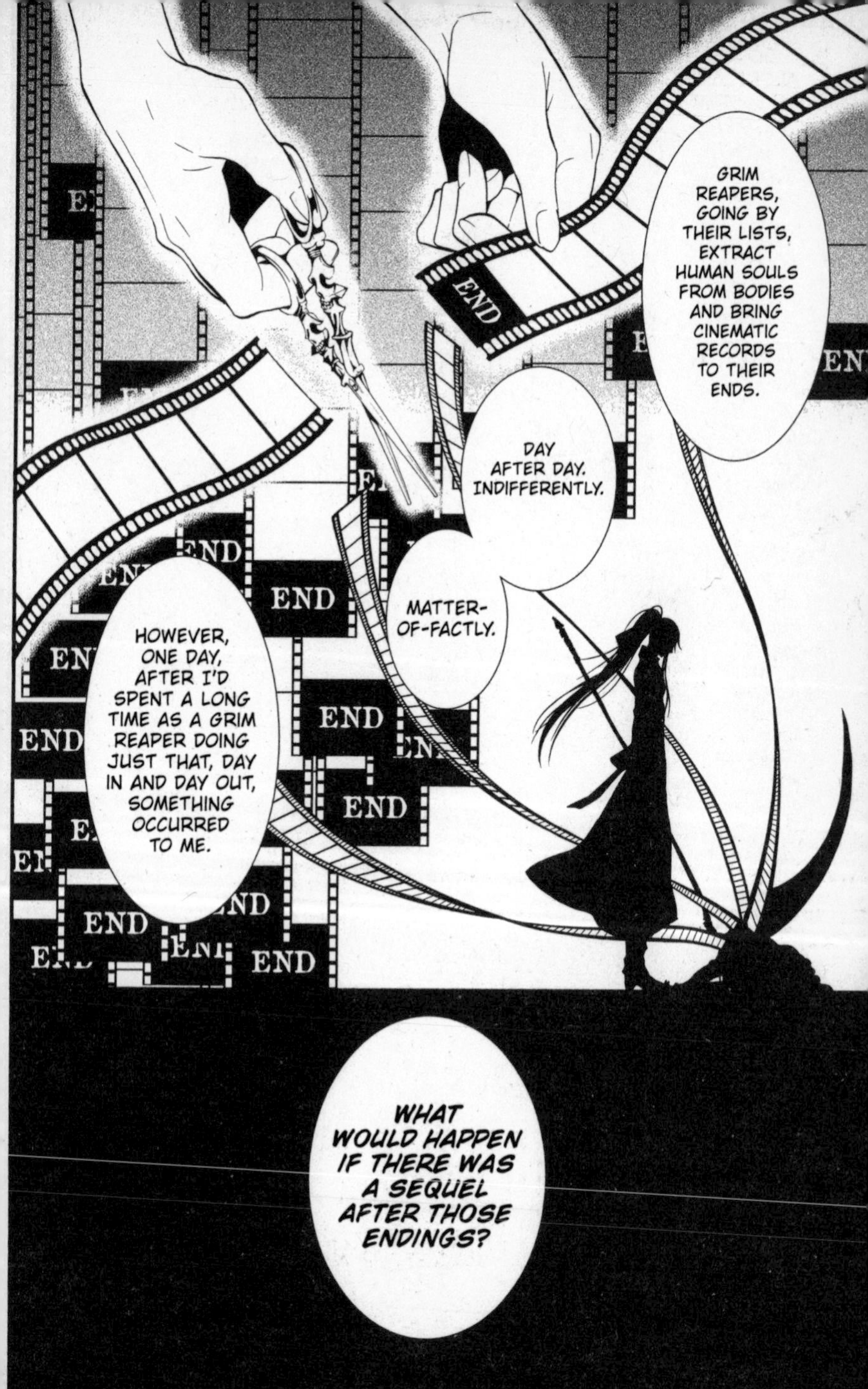
GRIM REAPERS, GOING BY THEIR LISTS, EXTRACT HUMAN SOULS FROM BODIES AND BRING CINEMATIC RECORDS TO THEIR ENDS.
DAY AFTER DAY. INDIFFERENTLY.
MATTER-OF-FACTLY.
HOWEVER, ONE DAY, AFTER I'D SPENT A LONG TIME AS A GRIM REAPER DOING JUST THAT, DAY IN AND DAY OUT, SOMETHING OCCURRED TO ME.
WHAT WOULD HAPPEN IF THERE WAS A SEQUEL AFTER THOSE ENDINGS?

SOULS ALONE ARE ALL GRIM REAPERS HUNT, AFTER ALL.

THE "BODIES" AND THE "MEMORIES" IN THEIR BRAINS STILL REMAIN *IN THIS WORLD.*

END

GrimReaper

WHAT WOULD HAPPEN TO THE BODIES OF FLESH THAT HAD LOST THEIR SOULS AND WHOSE MEMORIES HAD COME TO AN END IF I ***ADDED*** *A CONTINUATION TO THOSE VERY MEMORIES?*

!?

COME ON...
YOU'RE TELLING ME YOU EDITED THEIR CINEMATIC RECORDS?
WELL, NOW! WHY NOT USE YOUR POWERS AND HAVE A LOOK-SEE AT THEIR RECORDS FOR YOUR-SELF?
HEE! HEE!
おおおお
OOOO (MOAN)

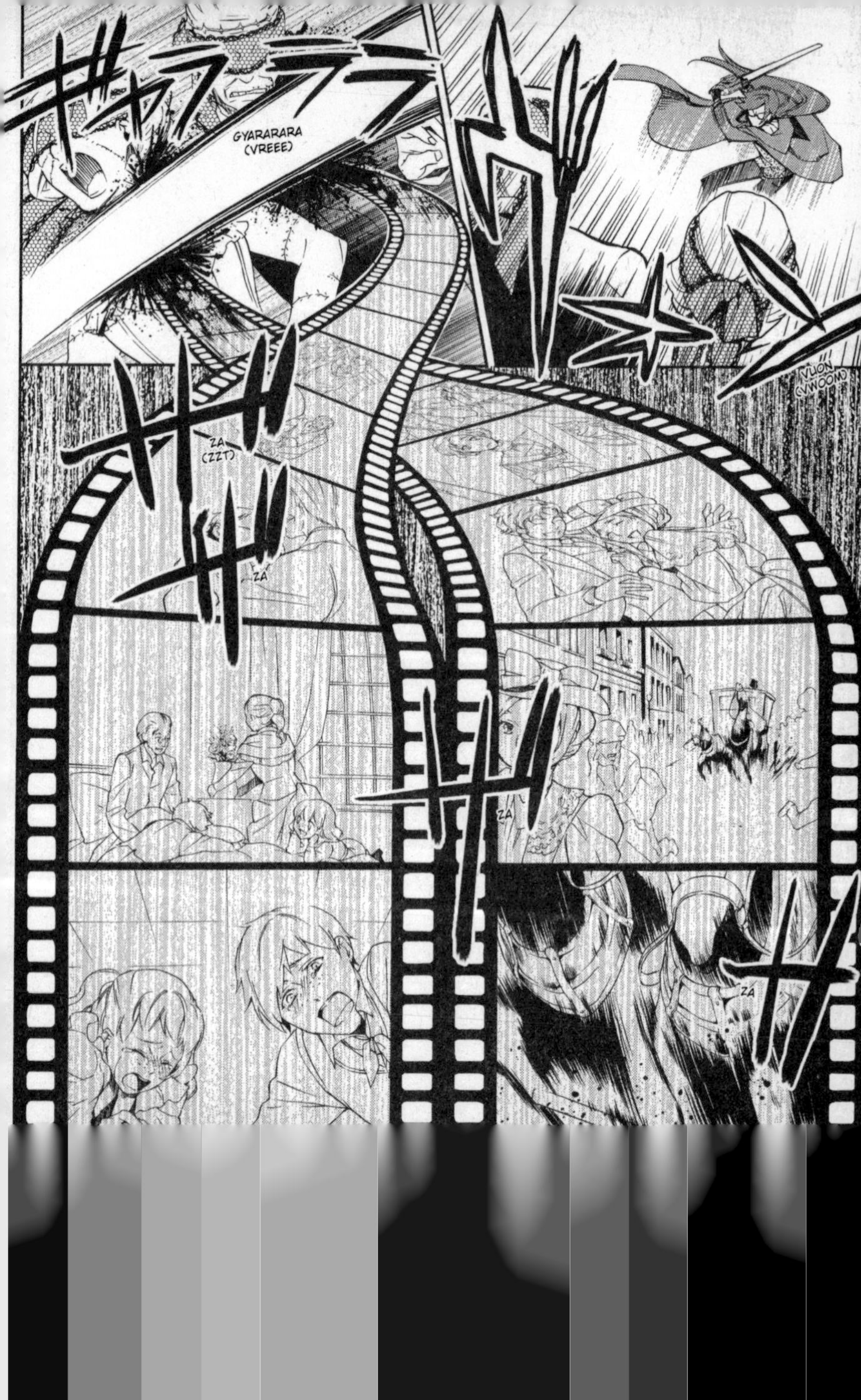
GYARARARA
(VREEE)
VUON
(VWOOM)
ZA
(ZZT)
ZA
ZA
ZA

PA (FLASH)
!?
ZA
HEY! WHAT IS THIS!?
ZA
THIS IS...!!
!?
CAN'T SEE
WHAT'S GOING ON!?
ZA
ZA

"THE END" TITLE OF A CINEMATIC RECORD, WHICH ARRIVES ARM IN ARM WITH DEATH...
END
...NEVER APPEARS BECAUSE I *ATTACHED* COUNTERFEIT MEMORIES TO THE RECORDS, LIKE SO.
AND TO MY SURPRISE...
...THE FLESH, UNDER THE MISTAKEN NOTION THAT "MY LIFE CONTINUES ON"...
...BEGAN MOVING AGAIN WITHOUT ITS SOUL!
!
ALL LIVING BEINGS INSTINCTIVELY ATTEMPT TO MAKE UP FOR WHAT THEY LACK.
IF THEIR BODIES ARE WOUNDED, THEY TRY TO CLOSE THEIR WOUNDS.
IF THEIR SPIRITS FEEL ISOLATED, THEY SEEK OTHERS TO ALLEVIATE THEIR LONELINESS.

SO *THEY* ALSO INSTINCTIVELY DESIRE WHAT THEY LACK...
AND IN SEEKING THEIR "SOULS," THEY ATTEMPT TO RIP OPEN THE BODIES OF LIVING HUMANS.

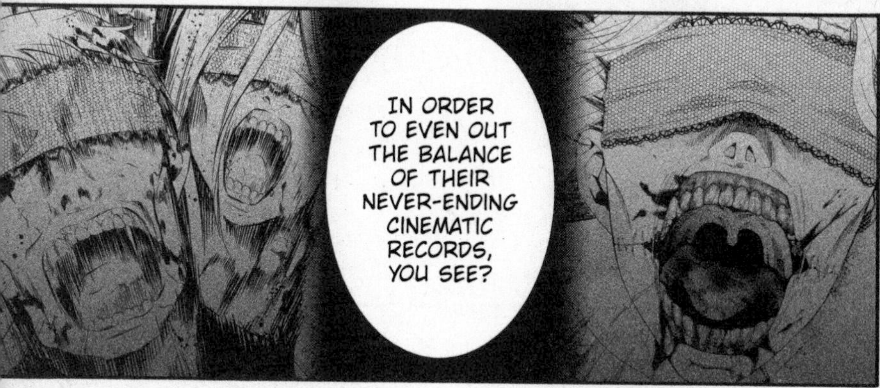
IN ORDER TO EVEN OUT THE BALANCE OF THEIR NEVER-ENDING CINEMATIC RECORDS, YOU SEE?

!

SO THAT'S WHY THEY CAME AFTER OUR SOULS WHEN THEY COULDN'T SEE OR HEAR US ...!?

EVEN THOUGH IT'S IMPOSSIBLE TO MAKE ANOTHER'S SOUL ONE'S OWN...

I CAN TAMPER WITH CINEMATIC RECORDS, BUT I CANNOT CREATE SOULS.
I EXPERIMENTED PLENTY, BUT MOST OF THEM BECAME NO MORE THAN DOLLS OF FLESH WITHOUT AN EGO.
AND SO I CALL THEM THUS—
NEITHER LIVING...
...NOR DEAD...
...THEY ARE "BIZARRE DOLLS," WARPED FLESH PUPPETS.
EVEN BAD TASTE HAS ITS LIMITS.
HEE! HEE!
IF YOU CANNOT UNDERSTAND THEIR BEAUTY, YOU HAVE QUIIIITE A WAYS TO GO, MY LORD!

WHITE, WAXEN SKIN THAT HAS BEEN SEWN TOGETHER PRETTILY IN SEMBLANCE OF THEIR LIVING SELVES.

MOUTHS THAT NO LONGER CLAMOUR LOUDLY OR SPIT OUT LIES.

ARE THEY NOT MORE BEAUTIFUL NOW THAN WHEN THEY DREW BREATH?

AUUH!

I'M GOING TO BE SICK!

THAT MAY BE HOW YOU FEEL, BUT...
...THERE ARE HUMANS WHO DESIRE THESE BIZARRE DOLLS, YOU KNOW?
!?

THESE CHILDREN DON'T FEEL ANY PAIN OR FEAR.
THEY SINGLE-MINDEDLY DESIRE SOULS AND DEVOUR THE LIVING...

WHAT SAY YOU?

DO THEY NOT MAKE THE BEST MILITARY ANIMALS?

THOSE ECCENTRIC FELLOWS SAID THEY WANTED TO SEE JUST HOW USEFUL *THESE* COULD BE...

...SO I DECIDED TO EXPERIMENT BY TOSSING THE SAME NUMBER OF "BIZARRE DOLLS" AS LIVE HUMANS ONTO THIS LUXURY VESSEL.

WHA—!?

...!?

WHO AND HOW MANY WILL BE LEFT STANDING WHEN THE KILLING ENDS?

...YOU REALLY HAVE LOST YOUR MIND.

HEE! HEE!
I NEVER IMAGINED WE'D RUN INTO AN ICEBERG, THOUGH.
HAVING QUIT BEING A GRIM REAPER, I DON'T HAVE MY LIST ANYMORE AND ALL...
WELL!
I'VE BEEN SAVED THE TROUBLE OF MAKING THIS SHIP SINK, SO IT'S A MATTER OF KILLING TWO BIRDS WITH ONE STONE!

I SEE.
SO...THIS PASSENGER LINER WAS NEVER MEANT TO SAIL TO AMERICA FROM THE BEGINNING.
BECAUSE OF YOU ALL, MORE HUMANS SURVIVED THAN I'D EXPECTED.
WILL I GET A SCOLDING FOR THAT?

HMPH.
THE MORE I HEAR, THE MORE WE CAN'T OVERLOOK THIS.
NO DOUBT.
IT'D BE MIND-BLOWING TO ALLOW A GRIM REAPER TO WARP "DEATH."

ALL THE SAME, HE AIN'T WEARIN' SPECS.
IS HE ONE OF THOSE "DESERTERS" WE GET ONCE EVERY BLUE MOON?

I DON'T CARE WHAT HE IS.
ANYWAY, A GRIM REAPER INTERFERING WITH LIFE AND DEATH IN THE HUMAN WORLD IS AGAINST THE RULES.
TO HEAR YOU OF ALL PEOPLE SAY THAT, SIR...
TYING HIM UP AND TURNING HIM OVER TO THE HIGHER-UPS WOULD ALSO SEEM TO BE THE MOST EFFICIENT WAY TO GET HIM TO REVEAL THE WORKINGS OF THE MOVING CORPSES, HMM...?
AND ...

...ON TOP OF YOUR BREACH OF CONDUCT, I SHAN'T FORGIVE YOUR SIN OF HARMING A GIRL'S FACE!

I SHAN'T FORGIVE YOU, EVEN IF YOU ARE A TOTAL DISH!!

GORUA (ROAR)

GYARARARA (VREEEE)
GARI (GRIND)
GARI
OOPSIE.
GARI
ZA (SLIDE)
I GOT YOUR BA—
DOKA (KICK)
DAAH!

BO
(VOOSH)
ZUZAA
(SLIIIDE)
HEY!!?

SEBASTIAN DARLING, WHAT DO YOU THINK YOU'RE DOING!?

GYU
(TUG)
WE CANNOT ALLOW YOU TO HAUL HIM AWAY.
HUNH!?

WE OURSELVES ARE TASKED WITH PRESENTING THE TRUTH BEFORE HER MAJESTY, THE QUEEN.
WE MUSTN'T LET HIM ESCAPE!
AND SO...
...WE SHALL TAKE HIM INTO OUR CUSTODY.

THIS IS A GRIM REAPER CONCERN!
THIS IS MY DUTY AS A BUTLER.
OUTSIDERS SHOULD STAY OUT OF IT!
MY!
I HUMBLY ASK THAT OUTSIDERS REFRAIN FROM INTERFERING.
MY...!

HA!
STOIC AS USUAL, SEBASTIAN DARLING! YOU DO KNOW HOW TO GET MY BLOOD RUSHING!

FINE, THEN!
IF YOU'RE RARING TO GO, WE WON'T HOLD BACK EITHER!

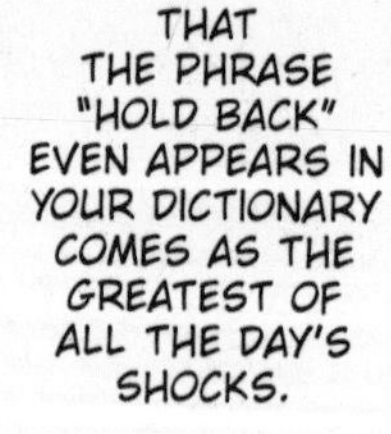
THAT THE PHRASE "HOLD BACK" EVEN APPEARS IN YOUR DICTIONARY COMES AS THE GREATEST OF ALL THE DAY'S SHOCKS.

YURA (SWAY)
THEN IT'S SIMPLE. THE FIRST ONE TO GET HIM WINS.

GIRO (GLARE)
AND I DON'T HAVE ANY INTENTION OF LOSING TO AN OLD MAN LIKE YOU!!

HEE! HEE...

THIS IS JUUUST LIKE RABBIT HUNTING.

...NOW, THEN.

WHO WILL BE THE HUNTED RABBIT?

DA
(LEAP)

Black Butler

Chapter 61

At night : The Butler, Born

BURORORO
(VROOOOM)
BO
(WHIZ)
!?
WHOA THERE!
MY MIS-TAKE!

BI (FLICK)
YOUR EYESIGHT SEEMS RATHER POOR...
IRAA (IRK)
...HM!?
WHOA!
GRIM REAPERS ARE ALL VERRRY NEAR-SIGHTED!
KA (SHNK)
KA
GYARARARA (VREEEE)
THAT PUTS YOU AT A DISAD-VANTAGE!!

GA (WHACK)

EH ...!?

I CUT THROUGH IT!?

THEN WHY COULDN'T I BEFORE!?

THE BLADE OF MY DEATH SCYTHE WON'T CUT THROUGH ...!?

NII (LEER)
—DO (WHACK)

GYARARA (VREEE)
TON (TMP)
...!!
GA (THWACK)
DAMN, MY SPECS!

YOU'RE STILL GREEN IF YOU'RE RELYING ON YOUR EYEEES!
GO (WHACK)

DO (THUD)
PASHI (SNATCH)
WHAT THE HECK ARE YOU...
...DOING!?
BI (TOSS)

THANK YOU, SIR—

ER!

BO (WHOOM)
KO (THNK)
GA (SHNK)
KA (CLACK)
MY, MY.
GA
GA
CAN YOU REALLY HUNT ME WITH SUCH TIIIIINY TABLEWARE, I WONDER?
GA
GA
BI (WHIZ)
THEY MAY BE INFERIOR TO DEATH SCYTHES, BUT...

KA
(SHNK)
KA
KA
...THE SHARPNESS OF OUR FAMILY SILVER IS FIRST-CLASS!
ZAN
(SLASH)

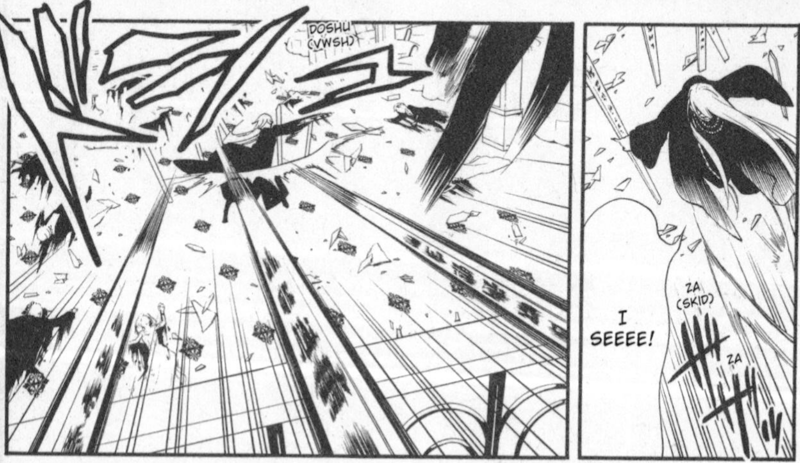
ZA
(SKID)
ZA
I SEEEE!
DOSHU
(VWSH)

COME, COME. WHAT'S THE MATTER? IS THIS ALL THE THREE OF YOU CAN MANAGE?
SUTO
(LAND)
YOU'RE GOING TO HUNT ME DOWN, AREN'T YOOOU?
HEE! HEE!

HE'S REALLY PISSING ME OFF ...
LET'S DO THIS QUICK.

THE SHIP IS LISTING PRETTY BAD.
WE'RE OUT OF TIME.

...YOU SAID IT.

DA (LEAP)

WE'VE GOTTA ATTACK HEAD-ON!!

GYARARA (VREEE)

I CAN'T BE WORRYING ABOUT MY LOOKS!!

GAKIIIN (CLAAANG)
GYARARARA (VREEEE)
AGAIN!?
I CAN'T BELIEVE THIS! A DEATH SCYTHE IS SUPPOSED TO BE ABLE TO CUT THROUGH ANYTHING...!
SO...
RARA

...HOW COME YOU CAN PARRY OUR DEATH SCYTHES!?
GYARARARA
THE DEATH SCYTHE CAN CUT THROUGH ANYTHING... HM?
DON'T YOU FIND THAT CATCHPHRASE A LITTLE FUNNY?
!?
WELL!
IT'S NOT FUNNY TO ME IN THE VERY LEEEAST!
GYARARA
HEE! HEE!

THERE IS ONE THING, ISN'T THERE?

ONE THING THAT IT CAN'T CUT THROUGH.

YOU DON'T MEAN ...!?

DOO (BOOM)

GAH-HAH-HAH...

DOSHA (WHAM)

......KUH ...!
ヨロ…
YORO (SWAY)

THAT'S A...

...DEATH SCYTHE!!

OOOOO
(WHOOOSH)
I SEE.
IN THE PRESENCE OF MANY DEATH SCYTHES, THE MOTTO THAT A DEATH SCYTHE CAN CUT THROUGH ANYTHING BECOMES A FALSEHOOD.
DON'T THEY GET COLLECTED UNCONDITION-ALLY WHEN A GRIM REAPER RETIRES...?
I FOUND IT HARD TO PART WITH MINE AS WE'D BEEN TOGETHER FOR SO LONG. 'TWAS SUUUCH TROUBLE SNEAKING IT OUT WITH MEEE!

NOW!
SHALL I TRY HUNTING YOU DOWN INSTEAD?
JUST LIKE THE PITIFUL RABBITS IN THE HUNT THAT YOU ARE?
ZUA (SWING)

DOO (WHOOM)
ぐら
GURA (SWAY)
ぐら
GURA
DO
DO (BAM)
DO
!!
DO
DO
DO
DO
DO
PASHI (SNATCH)

DO (BAM)
DO
DO
IT'S NO USE.
KIN (CLANG)

GOTO (CLUNK)
GOTO
SLICING TABLES IS NO DIFFERENT THAN BREAKING BISCUITS.
!

ZA (SLIDE)
I SIMPLY WANTED TO GET INSIDE OF THE WIDE REACH OF YOUR SCYTHE.

BO (WHOOM)

YOU THOUGHT UP AN AMUSING NOTION, MASTER BUTLER!

THEN ...

TO (TMP)

...I SHALL DO THE SAME.

!?

I CAN AT LONG LAST HAVE YOUR LORDSHIP SET FOOT INTO THE COFFIN I CUSTOM-MADE JUST FOR YOU...

ZA (ZOOM)

I KNEW YOU WOULD COME.

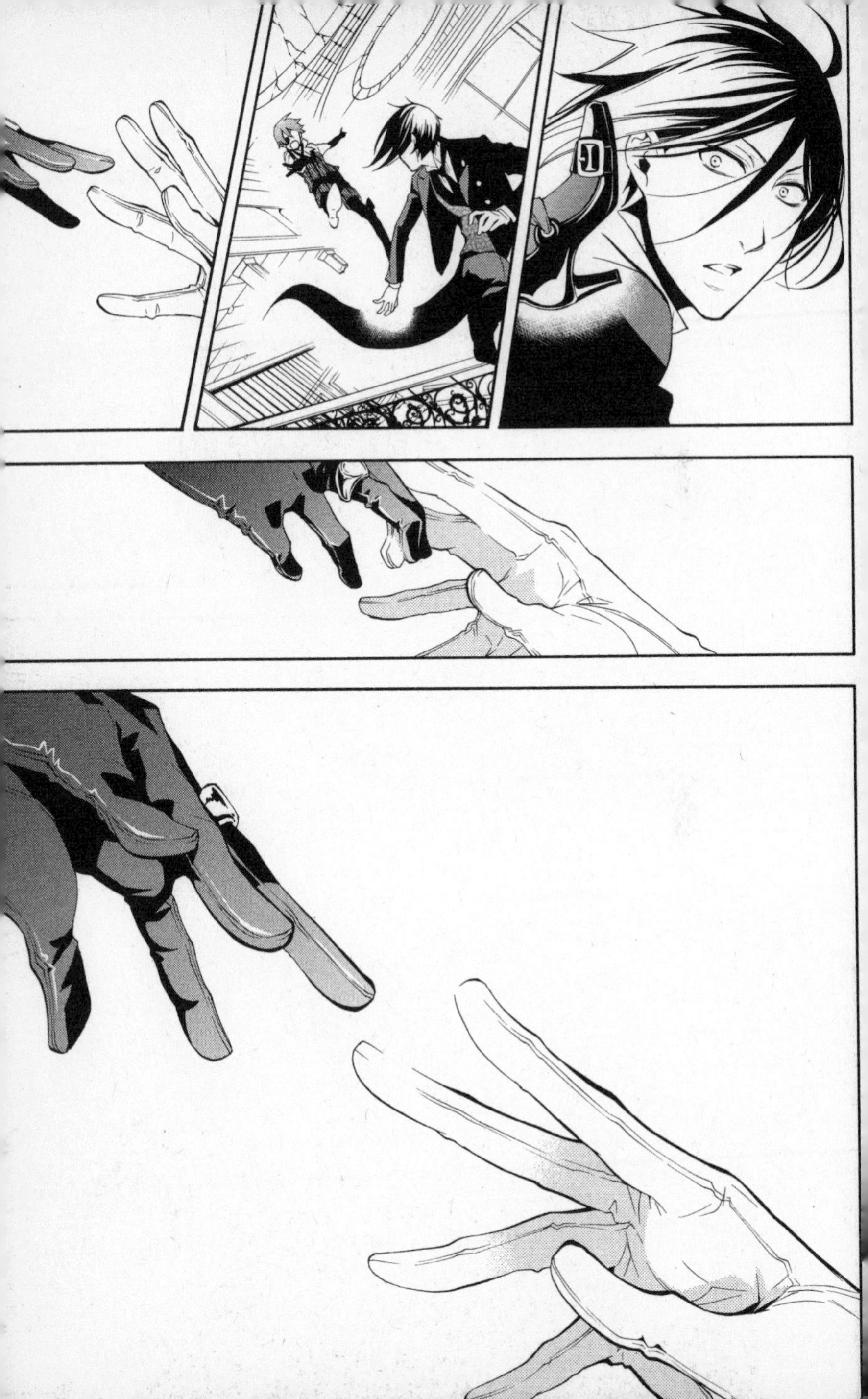

HUMANS ARE WEAK AND FRAIL, BUT IT IS SURPRIS-INGLY DIFFICULT TO DRAG ONESELF THROUGH A HUMAN LIFE...
...MASTER BUTLER.

YOU SEEEE, I'VE ALWAYS BEEN MOST CURIOUS ...

...WHY THE LIKES OF A NOXIOUS BEAST SUCH AS YOURSELF WOULD BE PLAYING THE PART OF A BUTLER IN A TAILCOAT.

I'LL HAVE YOU SHOW ME...
...YOUR CINEMATIC RECORD.

BUWA (BLAST)

SEBAS-
TIAN!!!

YES. HE IS CALLING ME.

AMIDST SORROW, RAGE, CONFUSION, AND DESPAIR...

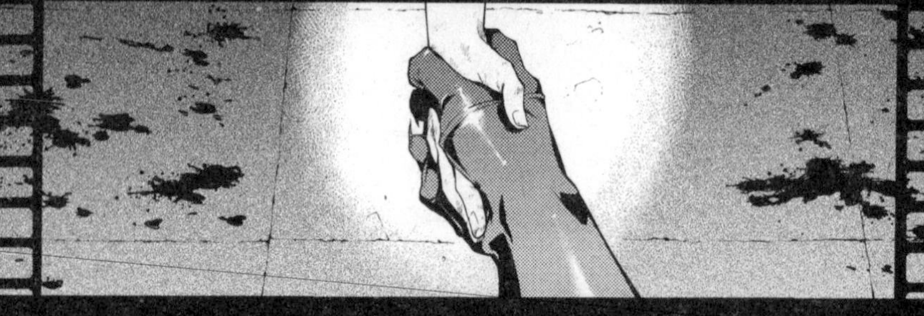

HE IS CALLING...ME.

WHAT IS YOUR NAME?

I AM...

......

CIEL.

CIEL PHANTOMHIVE.

THE SUCCESSOR TO THE TITLE OF EARL PHANTOMHIVE.
FU FU... I SEE. VERY WELL.
THEN I MUST TAKE A FORM BEFITTING THE SERVANT OF AN EARL.

コッ KO (CLICK)
—NOW.
コッ KO
COMMAND OF ME ANYTHING YOU WISH...
KO コッ

...MY
LITTLE
LORD.

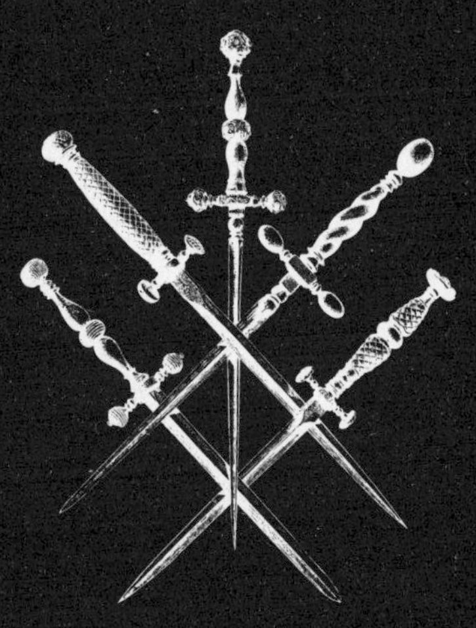

Black Butler

Chapter 62
At midnight : The Butler, Maturing

EEK!
KYAAAH!
I-IT'S REALLY COME!!
NO.

GRANT ME ETERNAL LIFE AND WEALTH!

NO.

—OH?

YOU HAVE MADE A GREAT SACRIFICE.
YOU ARE FREE TO DECIDE WHETHER TO MAKE A COVENANT WITH ME AND HAVE YOUR WISHES GRANTED OR NOT.
THE FEE FOR CROSSING HAS ALREADY BEEN WELL PAID.
GIRI (CLENCH)
I—
I...
...I WANT ...
...I WANT POWER ...
EEP ...!?
SOMEONE SHUT HIM UP!
ZAWA (CLAMOUR)
POWER TO TAKE VENGEANCE UPON THOSE WHO PUT US THROUGH ALL THIS!!

DEVIL!
I'LL MAKE A COVENANT WITH YOU!!
SO YOU WILL CAST OFF THE LIGHT AND CHOOSE THE ROAD TO HELL...
FINE.
THEN LET US CARVE THE MARK OF THE COVE-NANT ONTO OUR BODIES.
THE MORE CONSPIC-UOUS ITS LOCATION, THE GREATER THE POWER YOU WILL BE ABLE TO WIELD.
NOW WHERE DO—
ANY-WHERE WILL DO!

I WANT MORE POWER THAN ANYONE ELSE!!
YOUR SMALL FRAME BELIES YOUR IMMENSE GREED.
WELL, THEN!
THE MARK SHALL RESIDE ON THAT GREAT BIG EYE OF YOURS, WHICH REFLECTS A HOPELESS WORLD!

UWAAAA

AAAAA

GOOOOO (ROOOAR)

HE WISHED THREE THINGS OF ME.

TO PROTECT HIM WITHOUT BETRAYAL UNTIL HIS REVENGE CAME TO FRUITION.

TO OBEY HIS COMMANDS WITHOUT QUESTION.

AND TO NEVER TELL LIES.

ゴオ GOOO
FOR A BUTLER TO AN EARL TO EXECUTE THESE TASKS SMARTLY WILL BE NO EASY FEAT, I DARESAY.
オ...
THOSE WHO ATTEMPTED TO RUIN THE PHANTOMHIVE HOUSE ARE SOMEWHERE OUT THERE.
AUNT FRANCIS ONCE TOLD ME...
...THAT THE BEST CHANCE TO COUNTERATTACK IS WHEN THE OPPONENT MAKES THE FIRST MOVE.

ぎゅっ... GYU (CLENCH)

THE PREVIOUS EARL LOST THE GAME.

THIS TIME... I WON'T LOSE.

AS THE PRESENT HEAD OF THE PHANTOMHIVE FAMILY...

...AS CIEL PHANTOMHIVE... I WILL ABSOLUTELY NOT LOSE!

HEH HEH!

……
WHAT IS SO FUNNY?

NO.
IT IS JUST THAT YOU ORDERED ME NEVER TO LIE, BUT YOU YOUR-SELF ARE VERY MUCH A LIAR.

ギロ
GIRO (GLARE)

プイッ
PUI (FWIP)

OH, I SAY. WHAT A PAIN THIS IS.

—HOWEVER, EVEN THE FULL LENGTH OF ONE LIFESPAN OF A CHILD OF MAN IS BUT THE BLINK OF AN EYE TO ME.

I SHALL BE HAPPY ENOUGH TO KILL TIME FOR A SPELL AND THEN EAT MY FILL.

WELL, MASTER.
LET US RETURN TO YOUR MANOR.
I DON'T KNOW WHERE IT IS.

EH!?

I DON'T KNOW WHERE WE ARE, EITHER...
I'VE NEVER BEEN OUTSIDE OF THE MANOR MUCH...

I HAVE A RELATIVE AT THE ROYAL HOSPI-TAL IN LONDON.
WE WILL GO THERE FIRST.
UNDER-STOOD, SIR.

DEAR, DEAR...
I HAVE ENDED UP IN THE EMPLOY OF A SHOCKINGLY SHELTERED LITTLE MASTER WHO KNOWS NOT THE WAYS OF THE WORLD.

JUST A MOMENT, DEVIL.

WHAT IS YOUR NAME?

YOU MAY CALL ME WHATEVER YOU PLEASE, MASTER.

THEN...

SEBASTIAN.

YOU ARE SEBASTIAN AS OF TODAY.

VERY WELL.
THEN PLEASE ADDRESS ME AS SEBAS-TIAN FROM NOW ON.

WAS THIS THE NAME OF YOUR FORMER BUTLER, SIR?
NO...

IT WAS THE NAME OF MY DOG.

I RETRACT WHAT I STATED EARLIER.

I HAVE ENDED UP IN THE EMPLOY OF AN OUTRAGEOUSLY WICKED BRAT.

THE ROYAL LONDON HOSPITAL

ZAWA (MURMUR)

ZAWA

WOULD YOU PLEASE SEND FOR AUNTIE AN... RATHER, DOCTOR DALLES—

GASHAN (CRASH)

AH...
AAH ...!!
OLD MAN TANAKA !?
YOUNG MASTER ...! YOUNG MASTER!!
I AM GLAD...
I AM SO VERY GLAD TO SEE YOU ALIVE...!
—I SEE.
SO YOU DIDN'T CATCH SIGHT OF THE CULPRITS EITHER.
NO...

FORGIVE ME FOR FAILING TO PROTECT THE MASTER...

...... YOU'RE NOT TO BLAME, OLD MAN TANAKA.

......

YOU SAID YOUR NAME IS SEBASTIAN, SIR?

PLEASE TAKE THIS WITH YOU.

THIS IS?
SOME-THING THAT HAS BEEN PASSED DOWN THROUGH THE GENERATIONS OF BUTLERS TO THE PHANTOMHIVE HOUSEHOLD.

MISTER SEBAS-TIAN.

I KNOW NOT WHO YOU ARE, NOR WHERE YOU COME FROM, BUT I BEG YOU...
PLEASE TAKE CARE OF THE YOUNG MASTER.
...I SHALL.
AS HIS BUTLER, I SHALL SERVE THE *YOUNG MASTER* TO THE BEST OF MY ABILITY.
CIEL!!
AAH... YOU'RE NOTHING BUT SKIN AND BONE NOW!
I'M SO HAPPY ...!
YOU, AT LEAST, ARE SAFE...
......

THANK YOU FOR EVEN SEEING TO A CARRIAGE FOR ME, AUNTIE AN.

ARE YOU REALLY GOING? WHY NOT STAY WITH ME TONI—
NO, I'M GOING.

I WANT TO SEE IT WITH MY OWN EYES.

ぎゅっ…
GYU (HUG)

CIEL, I GIVE THIS TO YOU.

EVERYTHING ELSE WAS LOST IN THE FIRE. THIS WAS ALL THAT WAS LEFT.

...THANK YOU.

THIS... IS QUITE DREADFUL.
YOUNG MASTER?
FURA (STAGGER)

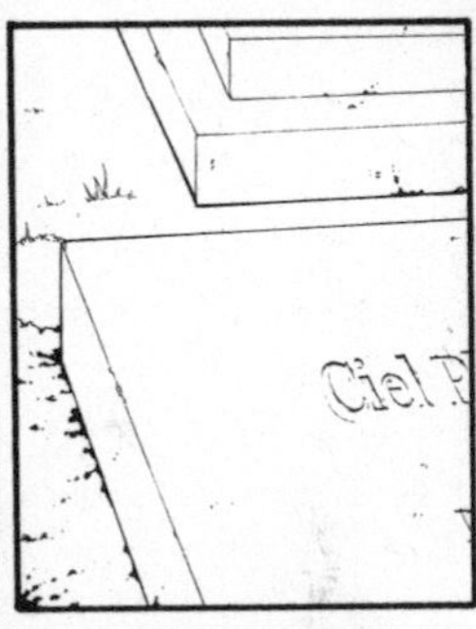
Ciel P

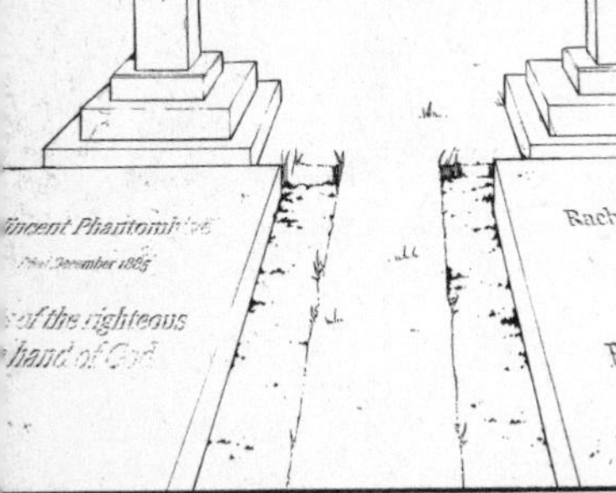
Rachel Phantomhi
Died December 18
We loved
But God love
incent Phantomhive
Died December 1885
of the righteous
hand of God

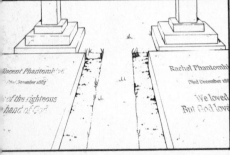

FATHER...
MOTHER...

THIS WOULD BE THE FIRST AND LAST TIME...

Vincent Phantomhive
The souls of the righteous are in the hand of God
...I HEARD HIM REFER TO HIS PARENTS THUS.

—NOW, THEN.

YOUNG MASTER.

THE SUN WILL SET SOON.
THE NIGHT AIR WILL BE HARMFUL TO YOUR HEALTH.

......
THERE'S A PLACE NEARBY WHICH IS BOTH A PUB AND AN INN, SO LET'S GO THERE FOR THE NIGHT—
ぱた
PATA (PAT)
PATA
ぱた

NO.
THERE IS NO NEED FOR THAT.

?

THIS CAN'T BE...
I SWORE TO YOU, DID I NOT? I WILL NOT LIE TO YOU.

H-HOW IS THIS EVEN ...?
I AM BUTLER TO AN EARL. IT GOES WITHOUT SAYING THAT I CAN MANAGE SOMETHING OF THIS LEVEL.

AND AN EARL MUST LIVE IN A GRAND CASTLE.

GII (CREAK)

COME.

THIS IS YOUR CASTLE FROM THIS DAY FORTH.

WELCOME HOME...

...MASTER.

HOHH!
HOHH!

HOT!!!!

BASASA (FLAP)
WHO IN THEIR RIGHT MIND WOULD POUR BOILING HOT WATER ON SOMEONE WITHOUT WARNING!?
AT LEAST CHECK THE TEMPERATURE FIRST!!
I BEG YOUR PARDON, SIR. I WILL TAKE MORE CARE NEXT TIME.
SO THIS IS TOO HOT...

GOSHI (SCRUB)
NOW IF I MAY, I SHALL BATHE YOU, SIR!
GOSHI
GOSHI
OUCH! OUCH! OUCH!
BASHA (SPLASH)
THAT WILL DO! DON'T TOUCH ME!
I'VE HAD ENOUGH! I'M GETTING OUT NOW!!
WHAT ARE YOU SAYING? YOU ARE STILL MIRED IN FILTH.
I WILL NOT STAND FOR YOU DROPPING DEAD SUDDENLY FROM AN INFECTED WOUND OR SOME-SUCH.

MUKAA (IRK)
...!
BASHA (SPLASH)
GET OUT!!

HFF!
HFF!
......AS YOU WISH.

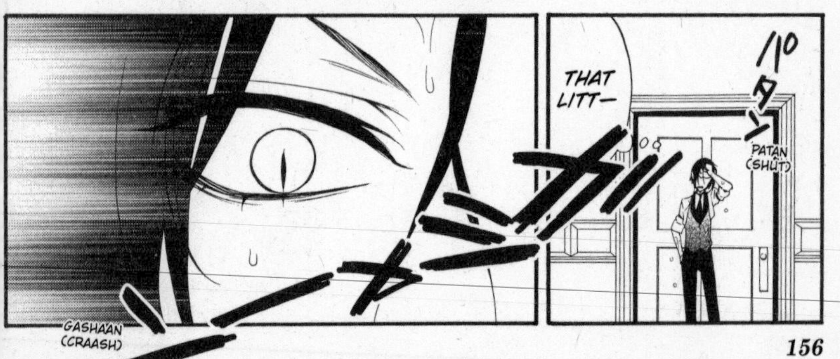
PATAN (SHUT)
THAT LITT—
GASHA'AN (CRAASH)

WHAT IS THE MATTER, SIR!?
!

......
はぁ〜
HAAA (SIGH)

よろ...
YORO (SWAY)
I SIMPLY SLIPPED WHILE TRYING TO GRAB A TOWEL.

YOU MUST BE EXHAUSTED FROM ALL THAT HAS HAPPENED TODAY... ALLOW ME TO WASH YOU DOWN.

ぱしっ
PASHI (WHAP)
I SAID NO.

!?
GA (GRAB)
IT WOULD DO TO KEEP YOUR OBSTINACY IN CHECK.
GIRI (SQUEEZE)
HUMANS ARE FRAIL ANIMALS. YOU CAN READILY LOSE YOUR LIFE FROM ONE PUNY GERM FINDING ITS WAY INTO THE TINIEST OF WOUNDS.
AS A CHILD WHO CANNOT EVEN SEE TO HIS OWN INJURIES, PLEASE DO NOT SEE FIT TO WASTE MY TIME.
....

GUUUU (GROOOWL)

HUMANS HUNGER MOST DISGRACE-FULLY UNDER ANY CIRCUM-STANCES.

...BE QUIET.

THEN, IF YOU WILL EXCUSE ME.

BASA (FLAP)
DON (BAM)
!?
GATA (CLATTER)
PLEASE EAT YOUR FILL OF WHATEVER YOU FANCY.

WE HAVE SPINY LOBSTER SAUTÉ AND ROAST TURKEY.
STICKY TOFFEE PUDDING AND FAIRY CAKES.
I SHALL SERVE YOU ANYTHING YOU LIKE.

...... SEBASTIAN.
YES, SIR?

DON'T EVER DO ANYTHING LIKE THIS SO CASUALLY AGAIN IN FUTURE.

WHY IS THAT?

AN ORDINARY BUTLER SIMPLY DOESN'T REBUILD A MANOR HOUSE IN THE SPAN OF ONE NIGHT OR HAVE DINNER PREPARED AT THE DROP OF A HAT.

IF ANYONE ELSE CATCHES SIGHT OF YOU DOING SUCH THINGS, IT WILL AROUSE THEIR SUSPICION.

THEN I SHOULD DO EVERYTHING STEP-BY-STEP AS MERE HUMANS DO?
I'M NOT TELLING YOU TO DO IT ALL TO THE LETTER, BUT AT LEAST *PRETEND* YOU ARE.
AVERAGE PEOPLE CAN'T MAKE ANYTHING WITHOUT THE NECESSARY MATERIALS AND TIME.

HOW TROUBLE-SOME.

YOU ARE MY BUTLER, AREN'T YOU?
DO AS I SAY.

UNDER-STOOD, SIR.
コトッ
KOTO (TOK)

ぱく
PAKU (CHOMP)

オエッ
OE (URP)
...!
UGH!!

OH? IS IT NOT TO YOUR TASTE?
GOKU (GULP) GOKU

SFX: PON (SMACK)

IT'S OILY, SPICY...
PUAH!
...AND SALTY...
AAH... AFTER HAVING SPENT SO MUCH TIME IN A PLACE LIKE THAT, THIS MENU MUST HAVE BEEN TOO RICH FOR YOU, YOUNG MASTER.
ぽん
GATA (CLATTER)
PERHAPS RISOTTO OR...
FORGET IT. I'M GOING TO BED.

......

KON (KNOCK)
KON
WHAT IS IT?
I HAVE BROUGHT YOU SOME WARM MILK.
YOU MUST HAVE SOMETHING AT LEAST...
I AM AWARE THERE ARE MANY OBLIGATIONS YOU MUST SEE TO FROM TOMORROW ON IN ORDER TO BECOME A SPLENDID FAMILY HEAD WHO WILL RESTORE THE EARLDOM.
I DON'T WANT IT.
I'M SURE IT TASTES AWFUL ANYWAY.

I HAVE ONLY HEATED UP THE MILK. I DID NOT ADD ANYTHING TO IT.
KOPOPO (POUR)
コポポ…
I CANNOT SPEAK TO ITS TASTE.

WOULD YOU CARE FOR SOME?

...IS THERE HONEY IN IT?

PLEASE, ADD HOWEVER MUCH YOU WANT.

OLD MAN TANAKA USED TO SCOLD ME, SAYING I'D GET CAVITIES IF I HAD HONEY BEFORE BEDTIME.

THEN I SHALL FOLLOW SUIT FROM TOMORROW ON.
FUU...
—MMM...

SEBAS-TIAN.

THE WARM MILK... WAS GOOD.

I AM GLAD TO HEAR IT.

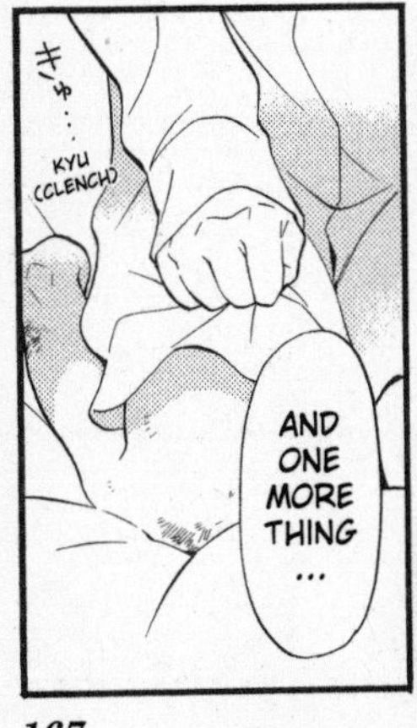
きゅ…
KYU (CLENCH)
AND ONE MORE THING
...

I WON'T FORGIVE YOU IF TOMORROW'S BREAKFAST TASTES AS FOUL AS WHAT I HAD EARLIER THIS EVENING.
TCH...
I DON'T MUCH CARE TO LIVE ON WARM MILK FOR EVERY MEAL LIKE A PUPPY.

PISHI (CRACK)

......VERY WELL.
GOOD NIGHT, YOUNG MASTER.

PATAN (SHUT)
......!

WHY, THAT LITTLE BLOODY KNAVE.

To be continued in Black Butler 14

Black Butler

黒執事

Downstairs

Wakana Haduki

7

SuKe

Saito Torino

Yu Kamiya

Tsuki Sorano

Nora

*

Takeshi Kuma

*

Yana Toboso

Special Thanks

Sakuya

for You!

Yana Toboso

AUTHOR'S NOTE

"I want to live like a tuna, which dies when it stops swimming." I want to tell the me, who made a comment like that in my debut manga, "Never stop, otherwise you really will die." Taking the first step after you've stopped and rested is a hundred times tougher than taking the very first step. The more you move forward, the more frightening it becomes to stand still. But I think this is like a runner's high, when I'm simply having fun running and don't want to stop. And so here's Volume 13, where I'm feeling like I'm leaning forward.

DOWNSTAIRS WITH BLACK BUTLER VI
YANA TOBOSO
LONG TIME NO SEEEEE!
THANKS EVER SO MUCH FOR BUYING VOLUME 13!
TOBOSO HERE!

THE LAST TIME I DREW "DOWNSTAIRS" WAS BACK IN VOLUME 7. TWO YEARS FLEW BY BEFORE I KNEW IT...
...AND BLACK BUTLER CELEBRATED ITS FIFTH ANNIVERSARY.
SO THIS IS WHAT I WROTE TWO YEARS AGO...
THANK YOU SO MUCH!

LOTS OF STUFF HAPPENED IN THOSE TWO YEARS.
EVERY ONE OF THEM WAS LIKE A DREAM...
A MUSICAL
FWAH, THEY'RE ALL GREAAAT ...!
SECOND SEASON OF THE ANIME
FOOD COLLABORATIONS IN NAMJATOWN

THERE'RE SO MANY THINGS I WANT TO WRITE ABOUT, WORDS FAIL TO DESCRIBE MY FEELINGS.
WHAT FILLS MY HEART NOW IS SIMPLY GRATITUDE TO THE STAFF INVOLVED IN ALL THE WORKS AND THE VIEWERS...
DVD

AND SO I'VE GOT NOTHING ELSE TO WRITE ABOUT.
DARAA (DROOL)
I DON'T GO OUT MUCH...
YOU'RE THE VERY PICTURE OF BURNOUT SYNDROME!

CAN'T YOU THINK OF SOMETHING? LIKE ANSWERING THE QUESTIONS IN YOUR FAN LETTERS.
OTHER MANGAKA OFTEN DO THAT.
NNN.
TO BE HONEST, THIS MANGA DOESN'T RECEIVE MANY QUESTIONS.
A LOT OF CHARACTERS AREN'T HUMAN, SO THEY DON'T HAVE BIRTHDAYS. THERE AREN'T ANY COMPLICATED FANTASY SETTINGS EITHER.
ONCE IN A WHILE, I DO GET REQUESTS LIKE, "PLEASE TEACH ME HOW TO DRAW HANDSOME MEN"...
I'M STILL DRAWING THE MAIN CHARACTER'S FACE BY TRIAL AND ERROR, PEOPLE!!!
BUT I'D LIKE TO KNOW HOW TO DO THAT TOO! DEATH-FINITELY!!!
KUWA (YELL)
I'VE ALSO GOTTEN "HOW CAN I BECOME A MANGAKA?"
STUFF LIKE THAT.
HA HA HA!
SO YOU'VE GOTTEN TO THE POINT WHERE PEOPLE ASK YOU THAT, HUH?
SEEERIOUSLY! I'M SURPRISED I MADE IT AS A MANGAKA MYSELF.
FU HEH HEH.
YOUR SERIES JUST HAD ITS FIFTH ANNIVERSARY, SO WHY DON'T YOU LOOK BACK ON EVERYTHING THAT'S HAPPENED SINCE YOUR DEBUT?
LET'S SEE...
I'D NEVER DRAWN AN ORIGINAL MANGA UNTIL I SENT IN MY WORK TO THE SQUARE ENIX MANGA CONTEST.
2003 OR SO
THE PROTOTYPE FOR THE GRIM REAPER DISPATCH—A MANGA FEATURING A PAIR OF GRIM REAPER BUDDIES (WEARING MILITARY UNIFORMS FOR SOME REASON -SMILE-)
THE WORK I SUBMITTED
HELL-O
KOUYA
GINJI
I DON'T HAVE THE MANUSCRIPT ON HAND, SO I ONLY REMEMBER IT REAL VAGUELY...
I NEVER STUDIED DRAWING EXCLUSIVELY OR WENT TO A PRO MANGA SCHOOL.
MY HIGH SCHOOL WAS AN ORDINARY SCHOOL.
HOWEVER, MY MANGA THANKFULLY CAUGHT THE EYES OF MISTER EDITOR K, AND HE BECAME MY EDITOR!
I RECEIVED THE ENCOURAGEMENT PRIZE.
THE CHARACTERS ARE SO-SO, BUT YOUR BACKGROUNDS AND STORY SUCK!!
WHAT HE TOLD ME RIGHT AFTER WE MET
—EH...!? OKAY, I'M SORR...

MY EDITOR TRAINED ME HARD, AND MY SECOND MANGA WAS ACCEPTED INTO THE SQUARE ENIX MANGA CONTEST...
BEGINNING OF 2004
...AND I FINALLY GOT TO DRAW A MANGA FOR A NEWCOMERS' ONE-SHOT PUBLICATION PROJECT!
AO
I ONLY HAVE FAINT MEMORIES OF THIS AS WELL.
KOHAKU
DISGUISE
THE WORK I ENTERED
WHEN I WAS DRAWING THAT ONE-SHOT, MY EDITOR CALLED ME OUT OF THE BLUE.
9TH
A STORY WHERE NINE PRINCES FIGHT A BATTLE ROYALE TO OBTAIN THE KING'S THRONE.
AROUND SEPTEMBER 2004
YES?
WE'VE GOT A PROB-LEM!
I WAS GOING TO PUBLISH YOUR ACCEPTED PIECE AS A ONE-SHOT IF THERE WAS SPACE IN THE MAGAZINE...
...BUT YOU'VE WRITTEN DIALOGUE IN THE GUTTER MARGINS!!!
WHEN I LOOKED AT YOUR FAXED ROUGHS, THE CROP MARKS WERE INVISIBLE, SO I COULDN'T TELL!!!
LET ME EXPLAIN!
A TWO-PAGE SPREAD IN A MANUSCRIPT
(CUT-OFF MARGINS)
HERE
MAGAZINES
THE GUTTER MARGINS ARE THE AREAS IN THE MIDDLE OF MANUSCRIPT SPREADS THAT ARE PUBLISHED IN MAGAZINES. WHEN THE MAGAZINES ARE BOUND, ANYTHING DRAWN OR WRITTEN THERE WON'T BE VISIBLE! SO WHATEVER'S THERE IS USELESS!!
EVERYONE WHO DRAWS MANGA KNOWS THIS. IT'S BASIC COMMON SENSE!!
AND IT'S NOT JUST ON ONE OR TWO PAGES! WHAT THE HELL WERE YOU THINKING!?
YOU DID IT ON ALMOST EVERY PAGE!!
EH? U-UM...
WHAT'S A GUTTER MARGIN?
EH...!?
EDITOR

YOU SHOULD AT LEAST READ A BOOK LIKE "HOW TO DRAW MANGA"!!!
I-I'M SORRY...
THIS IS REALLY BASIC!!!
I DIDN'T UNDERSTAND WHAT GUTTER MARGINS WERE, SO I COULDN'T QUITE UNDERSTAND WHAT I DID WRONG AND WAS FLUSTERED.
ORO (PANIC)
ORO

DESPITE WHAT HAPPENED, I JUST BARELY MANAGED TO FINISH DRAWING "9TH," MY DEBUT WORK.
I HAD TO REDRAW LOTS OF "9TH" TOO 'COS I'D DRAWN IN THE GUTTER.
FORTY-EIGHT PAGES...
AFTER THAT, MISTER EDITOR K AND I DEVOTED OURSELVES TO MANGA...
READ MORE MANGA. YOUR THUMBNAILS REALLY SUCK!!!
THUMBNAILS
READ MORE BOOKS TOO!!
R-RIGHT...
AROUND OCTOBER 2005
A SCHOOL BATTLE STORY FEATURING "FRIENDSHIP, ENDURANCE, AND VICTORY" BETWEEN A HUMAN WHO TRANSFERRED TO A MILITARY ACADEMY FOR VAMPIRES AND THE VAMPIRES THERE.
KEI
ALDRED
...AND AFTER I DREW MY ONE-SHOT SERIES RUST-BLASTER...
SEPTEMBER 2006
A CHAOTIC BUTLER MANGA
...BLACK BUTLER, MY FIRST LONG SERIES BEGAN.

BLACK BUTLER WAS ORIGINALLY SCHEDULED TO BE A SHORT SERIES, BUT THANKS TO EVERYONE'S SUPPORT, IT BECAME A LONG-RUNNING ONE.
CONGRATULATIONS. THIS IS GOING TO BE A LONG ONE.
I'LL NEVER FORGET THAT HANDSHAKE.
I FEEL BLACK BUTLER IS REALLY A MANGA THE READERS HAVE SUPPORTED FROM THE VERY BEGINNING.
THEN IT BECAME A DRAMA CD, AN ANIME (TWICE!), AND A MUSICAL. AND IN 2011...

...THE SERIES ENTERED ITS FIFTH YEAR... I GOT USED TO THE PACE OF DRAWING IT AND WAS FINALLY ABLE TO PROUDLY CALL MYSELF A MANGAKA... AND THEN!

TOBOSO SLAMMED INTO AN AMAZING FACT!!!

BAAN (BANG)

YOU GUYYYS —!!!

KA (YELL)

DID YOU KNOW...

WRONG PLACE TO INSERT THE NIB

GURA

GURA (WOBBLE)

CORRECT PLACE TO INSERT THE NIB

PISHI (STEADY)

...YOU'RE NOT S'POSED TO STICK THE NIB IN THE MIDDLE OF DIP PENS!!?

*HAS BEEN USING DIP PENS FOR ROUGHLY TEN YEARS

MOSTLY G-PENS

YES.

YANA-SAN, WERE YOU INSERTING THE NIB INTO THE MIDDLE ALL THIS TIME!!?

EH?

WELL, YEAH. 'COS THERE'S A SLOT IN THE MIDDLE!!

SEE?

CHIEF H

IF THERE'S A SLOT, ISN'T THAT WHERE YOU'D NORMALLY STICK IT !!!?

WASN'T THE NIB REALLY UNSTABLE !!?

YEAH, I'VE BEEN DRAWING THESE LAST TEN YEARS THINKING HOW UNSTABLE IT WAS.

ARE YOU STUPID!?

*WHILE DRAWING CHAPTER 58

AND I FOUND OUT A LITTLE WHILE AGO THAT MANUSCRIPT PAPER GETS DAMP, SO NOW I TAKE GOOD CARE OF MY MANUSCRIPTS.

JUNE

FOR SOME REASON, THE INK'S RUNNING.

HASN'T THE PAPER GOTTEN DAMP?

EH!? IT GETS DAMP!?

THAT'S ABOUT IT...

LOOKING BACK ON IT NOW, I'M EMBARRASSED.

HEH HEH.

HEY, THE STORY ABOUT THE PEN NIB AND ENTERING THE CONTEST SHOULDN'T BE IN THAT ORDER!

HOW TO USE YOUR PEN NIBS IS MORE BASIC THAN GUTTER MARGINS!!

BUT NONE OF THE BOOKS SAID ANYTHING ABOUT IT!

I READ THEM AFTER YOU YELLED AT ME!!!

IT'S NOT WRITTEN ANYWHERE 'COS YOU CAN TELL JUST BY LOOKING AT THEM!!!

WELL, THAT'S ME, TOBOSO, FOR YOU. BUT SOMEHOW I'M MANAGING TO GET BY AS A MANGAKA.

SEE YA!!

SO IF YOU KEEP DRAWING SERIOUSLY, IT'S POSSIBLE FOR ANYONE TO BECOME A MANGAKA. TO EVERYONE WHO WANTS TO BE A MANGAKA, DO YOUR BEST!!

Translation Notes

Page 3
Knifehand
The Japanese word used here is *tegatana*, or "knifehand strike," which is also known to many as a "karate chop." In this martial arts move, the outside edge of the hand, opposite the thumb, and the wrist are used to do physical damage to a target.

Page 13
Mourning period
Formal mourning was a complex social tradition for the upper classes in Victorian England. The closer one was to the deceased, the longer one was expected to be in mourning, especially if one was a woman. Being in mourning involved dressing in dark, somber clothing (often called "weeds") and all but retiring from society until the appropriate length of time had passed. Widows were expected to mourn for two years at the least, thereafter only gradually reintroducing color back into their wardrobes and themselves back into society. Coming out of mourning too quickly could be disastrous to one's reputation in polite society. Much of this tradition derived from Queen Victoria's lengthy mourning period after the passing of Prince Albert; after his death, she wore black for the rest of her life.

Page 53
Non
French for "no."

Page 53
Kaiser
A German title for "emperor" most commonly associated with the ruler of Germany between the years 1871 to 1918. The Holy Roman Emperors (962-1806) also used this title.

Page 53
Cock robin
This term comes most famously from the old English nursery rhyme, "Who Killed Cock Robin?", the subject of which is the murder of a robin and all the potential suspects who may have committed the crime.

Page 64
Undertaker's sticks
These "sticks" are called *sotoba*. *Sotoba* is the transliteration of the Sanskirt *stupa* (a tower that contains Buddha's remains), but in Japan, they usually refer to long, tower-shaped wooden tablets or markers that are erected beside graves. Sanskrit characters, posthumous Buddhist names, and other characters are written on them as part of a Buddhist ceremony for the soul of the departed. The kanji written on Undertaker's *sotoba*—南無大師遍照金剛—means "Faith in Koubou Daishi Kuukai." Kuukai is the founder of the Shingon sect of Buddhism.

Page 161
Fairy cake
A small cake for one person resembling a cupcake.

Page 171
Namjatown
Namjatown is an indoor theme park in Ikebukuro in Tokyo. They often have food collaborations featuring various anime and manga properties, such as "(X character)'s Parfait."

BLACK BUTLER 13

YANA TOBOSO

Translation: Tomo Kimura • Lettering: Alexis Eckerman

This book is a work of fiction. Names, characters, places, and incidents are the product of the author's imagination or are used fictitiously. Any resemblance to actual events, locales, or persons, living or dead, is coincidental.

Yen Press
Hachette Book Group
237 Park Avenue, New York, NY 10017

www.HachetteBookGroup.com
www.YenPress.com

Yen Press is an imprint of Hachette Book Group, Inc. The Yen Press name and logo are trademarks of Hachette Book Group, Inc.

First Yen Press Edition: April 2013

ISBN: 978-0-316-24429-9

10 9 8 7 6 5 4 3 2

BVG

Printed in the United States of America